DO NOT REMOVE CARDS FROM POCKET

CARD OWNER IS RESPONSIBLE FOR ALL
LIBRARY MATERIAL ISSUED ON HIS CARD

PREVENT DAMAGE – A charge is made for damage to
this book or the cards in the pocket.

RETURN BOOKS PROMPTLY – A fine is charged for
each day a book is overdue, including Sundays and
holidays.

REPORT A LOST BOOK AT ONCE – The charge for
a lost book includes the cost of the book plus fines.

LOS ANGELES PUBLIC LIBRARY

Form 36 2-65

NOV 4 1965

Administration of the Small Public Library

Administration
of the Small Public Library

Dorothy Sinclair

AMERICAN LIBRARY ASSOCIATION
Chicago 1965

PREFACE

The purpose of this book can best be indicated by a description of the reader for whom it is intended. The characteristics of the administrator of the small public library whom I have had in mind while writing are these:

He is charged with the administration of a library whose staff includes at most only one or two professional librarians besides himself. In other words, I have defined the "small" public library primarily in terms of staff. Size of community and book collection will vary.

He has a professional library education and probably some experience in the service aspects of librarianship. He knows the fundamentals of library theory and practice: reference books, catalog rules, and the like.

He is faced with many decisions for which his experience and training have only partially prepared him. The theories he has learned must be translated into practice, and much of his theoretical knowledge seems applicable only to larger libraries. In the small library considerable adaptation is necessary. He is introduced to some problems without even theory to fall back on. I have tried to assist the administrator in several ways: first, by identifying some of the managerial decisions that must be made; second, by emphasizing principles rather than specific practices; and, third, by encouraging long-range planning, the development of definite objectives, and the setting of priorities.

He is busy. With so small a staff, he cannot devote full time to administration and often is unable to provide the services he would like to give. I have tried to make this book practical, keeping in mind the realities of the administrator's working day. I have also stressed the small library's limitations and the resulting necessity of obtaining outside help from all available sources: the state library agency, library associations, and cooperative arrangements with other libraries, such as membership in a library system.

He is, probably for the first time, carrying the responsibility of a public official, charged with interpreting the library and its needs to his board, to other officials, and to the public at large. I have therefore included material which will help him in such presentations of library policy. Since more and more libraries are affected by centralized administration—city manager, civil service, or personnel board—I have given some attention to the situation of the librarian who works within such administrative patterns.

Obviously, a book of this type cannot treat every topic in detail. The bibliographies include references with fuller treatment. In some cases the works cited may not be slanted specifically to the small library. They are included because they are the only materials covering a topic or because they are the best available. As long as the small library administrator reads for general guidance and principles, rather than for specific instructions to be followed, he gains from knowing how a problem is handled in a larger library.

My thanks are due to Bill Katz, formerly of the American Library Association Publishing Department, for substantial assistance with judiciously applied prodding and encouragement as needed. Mrs. Dorothy Nyren gave the same kinds of help during the later stages of revision. I also owe a debt of appreciation to the colleagues—some unknown to me—who read and commented on the manuscript.

CONTENTS

1

LIBRARY OBJECTIVES: PROFESSIONAL STANDARDS AND COMMUNITY NEEDS

Library administration means decision-making. The chief difference between a head librarian and a library staff member is that the former is responsible, along with the board of trustees or other policy-making body, for final decisions about the way the library is managed. All administrators make long-range decisions, even when they do not recognize them as such. When a reader is granted or denied a privilege, when a piece of equipment is requested in the budget, when the back issues of a periodical are kept or discarded, decisions have been made that are far more important than the individual cases involved. If these decisions fit into the framework of a deliberate plan for library service and development, they are more likely to be consistent, logical, and wise.

Administrators of small libraries are not always experienced in planning. Many are undertaking their first professional assignments fresh from library school. Board members, as individuals, may be highly competent in other fields, but perhaps new to the ways of the library world and uncertain of their role in it. How, then, are librarian and board to function as the team that must make the best decisions for the library for which they are jointly responsible?

Decision-making based on good planning requires the long view. Busy people, concerned with many pressing details, find it difficult to make time to ask the searching questions that must be answered. But in the long run no expenditure of time is more important.

1

The First Decision—Library Objectives

Foremost among the questions librarian and board must ask, and the one on which all other questions will depend is, "What is the purpose of the library?" It is not enough to give a quick and easy reply, such as, "To supply books." The objectives must be clear enough to give direction to decisions on what kinds of books, how many, and for whom, as well as what kinds and amounts of service the library will offer. The search for guidance in working out an inclusive statement of purpose of the library will probably turn, on the one hand, toward the profession since it provides the knowledge on which the principles of librarianship are based and, on the other, toward the specific community the library serves since the principles must be applied within the framework of that community.

Spokesmen for the profession, as well as leaders in other fields who have studied the role of the public library, emphasize education as a major objective. They maintain that, if the public library is to deserve more than token support from public funds, it must give a service that the taxpayers and their official representatives recognize as important. In 1950 the social scientists who conducted the Public Library Inquiry stated that "the idea of a tax-supported institution such as the public library assuming the character of a general agency of out-of-school education is logically sound," and they found that the objective librarians themselves most often stressed was "to serve the community as a general center of reliable information and to provide opportunity and encouragement for people of all ages to educate themselves continuously."[1]

A more specific statement of public library objectives was made in 1956 by the committee of librarians, representing a variety of sizes and types of public libraries, who developed the public library standards:

Its [i.e., the public library's] function is to assemble, preserve, and make easily and freely available to all people the printed and other materials that will assist them to:

Educate themselves continuously
Keep pace with progress in all fields of knowledge

[1] Robert D. Leigh, *The Public Library in the United States* (New York: Columbia Univ. Pr., 1950), p.226, 223.

Become better members of home and community
Discharge political and social obligations
Be more capable in their daily occupations
Develop their creative and spiritual capacities
Appreciate and enjoy works of art and literature
Make such use of leisure time as will promote personal and
    social well-being
Contribute to the growth of knowledge.[2]

Thoughtful citizens, including public officials, join with professional leaders in emphasizing the library's importance in education. Gerald W. Johnson, in his introductory chapter to *Public Library Service*, states:

The public library is a way of escape from the narrow area of our individual lives into the field, finite, no doubt, but unbounded, of the wisdom and experience of all mankind. It is not the only way of escape, but for the majority of us it is by far the widest and the easiest to pass through . . .[3]

The U.S. Commissioner of Education, testifying before a hearing in 1963, called the public library "a basic educational resource" and added that

the widespread recognition that education is a lifelong process has dramatized the importance of having good public library service readily accessible to every citizen . . . Our national investment in good public library service is a direct and highly productive contribution to the intellectual life of our Nation.[4]

What do these general statements mean in terms of service to actual readers in actual libraries? They mean that the TV

---

[2] American Library Association, Public Libraries Division, Co-ordinating Committee on Revision of Public Library Standards, *Public Library Service: A Guide to Evaluation, with Minimum Standards* (Chicago: A.L.A., 1956), p.31. This publication will hereafter be referred to as the "standards" or as the "public library standards," since it represents the current statement of the profession on public library service of *minimum* adequacy. Administrators of some small public libraries may well be accustomed to think first of the *Interim Standards for Small Public Libraries*, described on p.8. This publication, and the standards it proposes, will be referred to as the "interim standards."

[3] *Ibid.*, p.ix.

[4] Francis Keppel, at a hearing before the Select Subcommittee on Education of the House Education and Labor Committee, April 9, 1963; quoted in *ALA Washington Newsletter*, April 16, 1963.

4

viewer who wants more information on Africa can locate it, that the businessman can obtain the latest work on personnel administration, that the drama group has access to not only plays, but also books on lighting and makeup. The scientist who wants to keep up with developments in his field finds what he needs; so does the youngster who is fascinated by space flight or dinosaurs. The public official uses his library to learn about developments in public finance and automation. And every citizen of any age is given the means to learn more about himself and his world, to read widely and deeply of the best that the past has produced and the freshest and best of today's writing and thinking.

Spokesmen for the small public library often react to such statements with a modest disclaimer. "For large libraries," they say, "this emphasis on education is fine. But we are a small library, supported by a small community. We cannot afford such ambitious aims. We try to provide good books that people enjoy, to encourage children to develop good reading habits, and to supply the reference books that are used chiefly by young people for schoolwork. That is about all we can manage. But we are proud of our library. We do well what we can do. We may not have everything the big libraries have, but we know our customers and give personal service. Ours is a friendly library, more so than the large, impersonal library can possibly be."

There is no denying that many small libraries do a fine job within their stated limitations. It is true that there are a warmth and a friendliness about the good small library that make it a pleasant and welcoming place. The large library finds it harder, though not impossible, to achieve an atmosphere of friendly welcome.

Limitations exist for every library, no matter how large. To accept inevitable limitations, and work within them for the best possible service, is the mark of a good administrator. But another duty takes priority; the librarian and board who are planning for community library service must inquire whether the present limitations *are* inevitable, and how seriously they restrict the library's value to its community.

The average citizen of the community served by a small library may be paying, on a per capita basis, just as much for library service as the resident of the large city, but he gets less for his money. The large library, supported by more citizens, can provide many more books, covering more subjects in much greater depth, than the small library. If people living in small communities were different from city dwellers, this differential in the value for the library dollar might not be a matter for concern. If all books were the same, like so many bars of soap or cans of soup, a smaller collection would be as adequate for the needs of a small population as the large library's resources are for the needs of its larger clientele.

But neither of these propositions is true. Books are not all alike, and people's needs and interests do not fluctuate according to the size of their communities. The average dweller in the small community has just as much intellectual curiosity as one in a larger city; his child takes the same courses in school as the city child. The old idea that rural or small-town people are backward or provincial has long been exploded. They are no less interested in world affairs and the arts, in broadening their horizons, investing their money, repairing their cars and refrigerators, purchasing wisely, decorating their homes, and guiding their children than are those who have access to a large library's greater resources on all these topics.

Is this inequity in what the individual's library dollar can purchase an unavoidable fact of life that must be accepted? Must the small library be content with more modest goals? Or is there a way in which the dweller in the small community can have library service that approaches the standards of larger libraries at a reasonable cost?

Achieving Objectives:
Library Standards and Systems

The committee of librarians who prepared the standards for public libraries issued in 1956 set down what it believed to be the minimum library service to which every individual in the country should have access. It began, that is, with the reader and not with the existing library pattern, recognizing that people's needs were not determined to any great extent by the size of the community in which they lived.

For example, among the standards given for library service of minimum adequacy are the following for library materials:

At least 100,000 volumes of currently useful printed material
4,000–5,000 separate titles added annually
300–400 periodical titles currently received
250 films, with at least 25 added annually

1,500 long-playing discs or recordings (not including duplicates), with 300 new records added annually[5]

Confronted with standards such as these, many small library
representatives throw up their hands, calling the goals completely
unrealistic. Yet the librarians who prepared the standards were
not cloistered dwellers in ivory towers; many of them were intimately acquainted with the small library's problems. They
knew that the average small community could not, alone, provide its citizens with the kind of library service described, and
offered the idea of library systems as a practical method of
achieving standards not individually but cooperatively.

Library systems exist not only in theory, between the pages
of *Public Library Service*, but in fact, in all parts of the United
States. The basic concept of library systems is sharing. Libraries
share their resources of books and staff so that the people of
each community have access to the resources of all. Many small
libraries operate successfully within the framework of library
systems and are thus able to expand their goals and offer their
readers more books and a far-richer variety of services than they
could otherwise.

Library systems take many forms: from informal cooperation,
through contractual agreements among independent units, to
complete consolidation. Patterns vary in different parts of the
country according to geography, custom, and preference. One
form of library system opens up the resources of a large city
library to its smaller neighbors under contract, and provides
certain centralized services from the city library as well. The
small libraries maintain their identities and continue to operate
with their own boards and librarians. They select their own books
as before but have, in addition, supplementary collections from
the system on a rotating basis. The system (which is distinct
from the large library) employs special consultants who help
the member libraries; for example, a children's librarian employed by the system will visit and advise the member libraries
about children's books and services. The small libraries help by
serving border residents of the city and sometimes patrons of
other small library members of the system.

[5] American Library Association, Public Libraries Division, Co-ordinating
Committee on Revision of Public Library Standards, *op. cit.*, p.36.

Another fairly common type of system is composed of small and medium-sized libraries. Since there is no one major resource, it is important that each library have access to the collections of all; thus close communication, efficient methods of transportation, and reciprocity of borrowing privileges are necessary. The libraries may agree to stress different subjects in their collections, so that the system as a whole will have better-than-average collections in several fields of knowledge important in the area. Systems of this type may collectively own and circulate films, employ consultants, and perform for all the libraries services that can be centralized, such as ordering, cataloging, and preparing books for use. These are only two of the many types of library systems that are giving good library service to many Americans.[6]

While it is easy to see that such sharing gives more patrons access to a wider variety of books and to the services of staff with special skills, the question is sometimes asked whether it does not tend to destroy the unique qualities of the small library already mentioned as its great advantages: its warmth, friendliness, and close acquaintance with its readers. This is a serious question, as these values are important and worth preserving. It might be argued that a larger collection and staff outweigh the human qualities the small library cherishes, but many question whether these qualities must be sacrificed in order to gain the advantages of the larger organization. Can the small library both gain the expanded resources of a regional system and maintain the human qualities that it cherishes?

Experience has proved that local interest, support, and pride are indeed worth striving to keep. New patterns of library cooperation now being developed stress them. Centralized systems are making special efforts to include representatives of each community in planning and to provide for local differences and specializations. What is important to the small library is important to the system, too. Local librarians and trustees usually discover that they can provide much better library service for

---

[6] Descriptions of the operations of existing library systems may be found in the following: Harold S. Hacker, "A Federated Library System in Action," *News Notes of California Libraries,* 54:247-61 (Summer, 1959); Edward Locke, "The Small Library: Thinking Big," *Wilson Library Bulletin,* 37:780-81 (May, 1963); Edward B. Hall, "The Southern Maryland Regional Library Association," *Maryland Libraries,* 28:8-9 (Winter, 1962).

their readers through system membership with no inconvenience or loss to the reader himself.

The decision about system membership is one of the most important facing the small library today. It must be made locally and based on local needs. Like all major decisions, it should be made only after careful investigation and as a part of total library planning. Failure to decide is, in itself, a decision not to take into account one of the major trends in modern library practice. Will system membership help the library to give better service to this particular community?—that is the only question that matters. A farsighted answer may well make possible a dynamic revision of library goals and a realization that the standards are not, after all, unattainable.

Working toward Objectives: Interim Standards and Guides

While system membership is the profession's first recommendation to the small library in its search for a way to expand its objectives and services, not every small library can enter a system immediately. There may be no system available near at hand, or there may be legal obstacles or other problems. Developing a system where none exists may be a long-term project. The standards in *Public Library Service* are based on the supposition that systems will come into being where they do not now exist. *Interim Standards for Small Public Libraries*[7] was formulated to serve two purposes: first, to set goals of achievement for small public libraries within systems and, second, to outline for small public libraries outside of systems intermediate goals as first steps toward the attainment of adequacy.

Interim Standards stresses the library's educational role and, in addition, urges that "the program of each public library should focus upon clear and specific objectives."[8] Definite qualitative and (where appropriate) quantitative standards are given toward which the smaller library may realistically work, if it has not already reached them.

[7] American Library Association, Public Library Association, Subcommittee on Standards for Small Libraries, *Interim Standards for Small Public Libraries: Guidelines toward Achieving the Goals of* Public Library Service (Chicago: A.L.A., 1962). 16p.
[8] *Ibid.*, p.5.

Another professional aid for the small library trying to raise its sights is offered by the pamphlets published by the Small Libraries Project of the American Library Association. These brief guides, with their practical supplements, are intended for the smallest libraries—those serving populations of under 10,000— but have been found useful by librarians and boards serving larger populations as well. The beginning administrator will find in them helpful "how-to" guidelines in his effort to translate what he has learned in library school into practices that are feasible and effective in the small library he is called on to direct.[9]

Reaching Objectives That Exceed Standards

In the foregoing comment on achieving and working toward objectives, it has been assumed that the small public library, operating independently, will have difficulty in achieving the goals described and the standards set forth in *Public Library Service*. For most small libraries this assumption is probably true. The emphasis on cooperation and systems in the standards, however, does not imply that it is impossible for the independent small library to achieve standard service. Some small libraries, with aggressive leadership and strong community support, have proved that it can be done. For libraries which meet or approach standards, either independently or within systems, a word of caution may be necessary. The standards state criteria for library service of *minimum* adequacy. The framers of the standards did not intend them as ultimate goals. No library, however fine or fortunate, can afford to assume that there is no room for improvement. No board can relax after a commendable effort has brought library service and support up to minimum standards.

Community-centered Objectives

In turning to the profession for help in formulating objectives the librarian and board of the small library receive, then, three guidelines: (1) agreement that objectives are important,

[9] Individual pamphlets in this series of sixteen, as well as some of the supplements, are listed in the bibliographies following this chapter and later ones. A complete list, and the pamphlets themselves, may be obtained from the Library Administration Division at American Library Association Headquarters.

(2) encouragement to emphasize the broadly educational purpose of the library, and (3) suggested methods of achieving broader objectives through system membership, or, while working toward system membership and the goals of *Public Library Service,* use of the interim standards. If the librarian and board can agree that educational service is to be a major concern, they have made their first important decision. Having reinforced their conviction that library service does matter, they should be able to work vigorously to make it what it ought to be, and they should not be timid or modest in putting forward its claims for community support and official recognition. Even then they will not have completed their task of formulating objectives, however, for their purposes and plans must still be related to their own community.

It is possible to imagine a library planned in a sort of vacuum: a copy of a successful library building could be erected, a book collection purchased from some standard list, a staff brought in according to an accepted classification plan, furniture purchased from a supplier's catalog. Service could be given in such a library, but it would be far from ideal because it would not be directly related to the community served.

To plan good library service policy makers must look closely at the community. The building, the staff, the book collection, the kinds and amount of service—all must be tailored to it. It is important to distinguish between relating library service to a community's needs and scaling it down to a community's size. As has already been noted, people in small communities are not different in any essential respect from those in larger ones. Community-centered library service is concerned not with size, but with the features that make each community different from any other, features that often have no connection with census figures. For example, New York must provide for many Puerto Ricans; Detroit, for many automobile workers. Similarly, the small suburban community with little industry must provide for garden lovers and pet owners to a greater degree than the library serving an industrial suburb. The latter, in turn, will need a different type of vocational material. The librarian and board, in assessing their own community, will seek not the basic human needs and interests that exist everywhere, but the special local needs and interests that call for fulfillment. Only thus can they provide a library service that is right for *this* library serving *this* community.

The first step toward community-centered service is the gathering of facts about the community itself. Many librarians and boards will feel, with some justification, that they have all the facts they need. Years of living and working in a community do, of course, supply a familiarity of a special kind. Such familiarity, however, has its shortcomings and has been found to be most useful when supplemented by factual and objective information from other sources.

Most people live and work in their own circles. These circles may overlap those of others at some points, but may miss many groups altogether and touch others only superficially. As a public agency the library has an obligation to know the interests and needs of all the people and to consider its service pattern with these facts in mind. If it must emphasize some aspects at the expense of others—and most libraries are faced with such choices—it ought to do so only after all the facts are in and all the factors carefully considered.

One natural but questionable tendency of librarians is to assume that readers who now use the service are more or less identical with "the community" and that what they ask for is a true indication of the community's needs and interests. These assumptions take much for granted. The librarian and board must ask why others do not use the library, whether it is because they cannot or will not, or because the library is failing to provide what they would use. Many a librarian who has hesitated to buy a particular book or subject because there was "no demand" has been surprised to find the book or material has been used when provided. Frequently the response has been a delighted "I didn't know that the library had such books" from a veteran reader.

How many readers do not know "the library has such books" and therefore do not ask for them? Perhaps demand is conditioned by an idea of the public library that is inadequate because the library itself, or possibly a library used previously in another community, has been inadequate. Perhaps readers have come, been disappointed, and failed to come again, at least for a particular type of service or material. The demand-oriented library, unless the demand springs from a well-informed public with a high standard of public library service, is giving only partially community-centered service.

To supplement the knowledge the librarian gains from personal experience in and out of the library, therefore, facts are needed. Fortunately, most communities have many sources available for such facts. Some of the facts needed are:

Age levels and proportions. How many children? young adults? older people? members of minority groups?

Education. How many with college or graduate degrees? what other educational levels? How many attending special classes for additional education or brush-up work?

Economic facts. Occupational patterns, industries, small businesses, farms, numbers of skilled and unskilled workers and professions

Schools and colleges. Existing educational facilities, including specialized, vocational, and remedial institutions, public and private

Community habits. Size and type of home, popular recreations and interests

Cultural opportunities. Regular concerts, theaters, lectures, amateur groups, and the like

Civic interests and problems. Patterns of community growth, needs for expanded facilities, matters of public concern

Churches. How many? what denominations? how large? How many have weekday group meetings, discussion groups, summer programs for children?

Clubs and organizations. Service clubs, special interest and hobby groups, book and current affairs discussion and action groups, civic groups, senior citizens, neighborhood clubs, Scout troops

Institutions. Hospitals, health and welfare institutions

The sources which may be available locally include:

U.S. Census, especially tract or district records, which give considerable information

School records

Local chamber of commerce, or equivalent

Planning department of the community or region

Agricultural sources (Grange, Farm Bureau, farm and home extension agents)

Published directories of business, industry, national organizations with local units

Card files of organizations (many libraries keep their own card files of community organizations and officers. This is a useful practice if such a file is not kept elsewhere, avail-

able not only to the library for its own use but also to its
readers)

Newspapers, especially local and regional ones, which give
details of meetings, projects, and new organizations

Personal interviews with representatives of organizations,
institutions, and businesses. These have an added value
in making friends for the library and creating an opportunity to talk about its services

When all these sources of information have been tapped, the
librarian, board, and staff have a sound, factual foundation to
which to add their own personal knowledge of the community.
While this personal knowledge should not stand alone, it is
indispensable. Each staff member and each trustee contributes
his own familiarity with the community to the total sum of information. The value of each contribution often depends on the
degree of participation in community affairs. Ideally, someone
connected with the library should be active, as a citizen, in
every community effort of importance.

Total participation is not always a realistic possibility. For
example, while it is particularly valuable for the librarian who is
a newcomer to participate in community activities and organizations, both to become known and to learn, this enjoyable part
of his job must be balanced with other work, reading, and personal interests. The busy organizational life of the normal lively
community can exhaust the librarian who is too much of a join-
er, to the extent that he has less to give in the long run to the
library and community alike. The staff ought to share, and the
board ought to share. And if, as may well happen, the community is so active that complete coverage is a burden, it is better
that those connected with the library participate with enthusiasm and zest in fewer activities than that they attempt to include all activities at the expense of relaxation and personal
health, physical or mental.

The important thing is that they do participate, that they add
to their objective knowledge of the community that indispensable
touch of inside knowledge. They will then be supplied not only
with the facts but also with the feel of the unique complex of
humanity that is their own community.

Having learned what is distinctive about their own community, they need next to learn what it has in common with others.
All small communities are alike in some ways, though each has

14

its special characteristics and charms. Therefore, just as other officials learn with benefit how the traffic problem or juvenile delinquency has been handled elsewhere, so librarians and trustees need to "talk library" with librarians and board members in communities like their own, to visit, to observe, and to read.

When librarian, staff, and trustees have considered their library against the background of a study of the standards and principles of librarianship and a study of their own community as compared to other communities, they will have achieved a sound basis for establishing policies and for making practical day-to-day decisions. They will have a clearer vision of what the library's objectives should be, because they are now wearing the library equivalent of bifocals. Through knowledge of general professional standards, they can see more vividly the long-range, broader picture; through community study, they have a better-focused vision of the needs close at hand. Although the spectacles may not be rose-colored, they show more clearly the road ahead.

Bibliography

Martin, Lowell. "The Twentieth Century Concept of Public Library Service," in Roberta Bowler, ed., *Local Public Library Administration,* p.1–8. Chicago: International City Managers' Assn., 1964.

Richardson, Ransom L. "Small and Medium-sized Public Libraries," *Library Trends,* 10:132–38 (October, 1961).

Rose, Ernestine. *The Public Library in American Life.* New York: Columbia Univ. Pr., 1954. 238p.

Wessels, Helen E. *The Public Library: A Tool for Modern Living.* (Small Libraries Project Pamphlet, no.1) Chicago: A.L.A., 1962. 8p.

Standards and Cooperation

American Library Association. Public Libraries Division. *Cooperative Practices among Public Libraries.* (PLD Reporter, no.5) Chicago: A.L.A., 1956. 70p.

———— ———— Co-ordinating Committee on Revision of Public Library Standards. *Public Library Service: A Guide to Evaluation, with Minimum Standards.* Chicago: A.L.A., 1956. 74p.

———— Public Library Association. Subcommittee on Standards for Small Libraries. *Interim Standards for Small Public Libraries: Guidelines toward Achieving the Goals of Public Library Service.* Chicago: A.L.A., 1962. 16p.

Duchac, K. F. "Service-centered Cooperation," *Maryland Libraries,* 28:6–7 (Winter, 1962).

Lorenz, John G., and Vainstein, Rose. "Emerging Trends of Library Organization," in Roberta Bowler, ed., *Local Public Library Administration,* p.26–49. Chicago: International City Managers' Assn., 1964.

Sabsay, David. "The North Bay Cooperative Library System," *News Notes of California Libraries,* 58:335–47 (Summer, 1963).

Smith, Hannis S. *Cooperative Approach to Library Service.* (Small Libraries Project Pamphlet, no.16) Chicago: A.L.A., 1962. 12p.

Library and Community

American Library Association. Library Administration Division. Small Libraries Project. *Our Library: What Is It Doing? Where Is It Going? A "Do-It-Yourself" Survey for the Small Library.* (Supplement A to Pamphlet no.14) Chicago: A.L.A., 1962. 7p.

———— Library Community Project. *Studying the Community: A Basis for Planning Library Adult Education Services.* Chicago: A.L.A., 1960. 128p.

Claff, W. L. "Two Way Street: The Public Library and the Community," *Bay State Librarian,* 51:11–12 (October, 1961).

Foster, Edith. *The Library in the Small Community.* (Small Libraries Project Pamphlet, no.14) Chicago: A.L.A., 1963. 8p.

Phinney, Eleanor. "The Extent and Quality of the Library's Adult Educational Program: An Outline for Self Study," and "Observing a Library Program," in her *Library Adult Education in Action,* Appendix A, p.148–61, and Appendix B, p.162–67. Chicago: A.L.A., 1956.

Severns, Hannah. "The Community-centered Library," *Pennsylvania Library Association Bulletin,* 19:23–25 (May, 1964).

2

LIBRARY LAW,
MANAGEMENT, AND FINANCE

Along with the important task of becoming acquainted with the community, the librarian must become familiar with the official framework in which he operates as an administrator. To make full use of his professional knowledge, to be able to put into effect his plans for development of library service, he needs considerable practical information. The public library is an agency of local government, regulated by law and subject to a variety of rules and obligations. The librarian must learn how to use prescribed procedures, how best to accomplish within the existing framework what he wishes to do. It is a mistake to dismiss regulations as so much red tape. The wise librarian knows that, in the long run, the book collection and the readers benefit when he possesses the legal and civic knowledge of an effective public official.

The Library's Legal Basis

The government of the public library, like all government, rests on law, regulation, and custom. Normally, libraries are set up in accordance with state legislation of the "enabling" type—that is, it is permissive rather than mandatory law which, while not requiring the establishment of libraries, lays down conditions for their operation where they exist. State library laws vary considerably in the amount of detail included.

Frequently local ordinances and regulations supplement the state law. These may spell out in more detail the way the library is governed locally but must be consistent with state legislation, except where a home rule charter has been granted by the state.

16

The librarian must be aware not only of the law itself but also of its interpretation, and must understand the different levels at which interpretation may occur. Thus:

1. The interpretation of a local legal officer is binding on a library, unless superseded by
2. The interpretation of the legal officer of the state, handed down in an official opinion, which is binding unless superseded by
3. The decision of a court in an actual case, which is binding unless superseded by one of the following:
4. The decision of a higher court, or
   The later decision of a court at the same level presenting a different interpretation which has equal weight but not necessarily more, or
   New legislation

Custom, or administrative practice, has almost the force of law in many localities when it is not in conflict with an actual statute, ordinance, opinion, or decision.

It is of utmost importance that the librarian and trustees of any public library be familiar with the law in all its various aspects. The law indicates not only what must and what must not be done, but also what may be done. Frequently, acquaintance with the law and local government procedures will open up new possibilities for action by the librarian. Legislation passed to enable a public hospital or the public schools to accomplish some objective may, for example, be general enough to apply to the library, and thus enable the library to function in a way formerly impossible. State library agencies, which keep informed on state legislation affecting libraries, are able to advise the local librarian of pertinent provisions. State agencies as a rule also publish convenient compilations of the state library laws, and state library consultants are familiar with the ways in which the law is interpreted throughout the state. The local legal officer is another source of information and advice.

With the increasing participation of the federal government in library financing, the local librarian cannot neglect attention to federal library-related legislation. In addition to the obvious laws such as the Library Services and Construction Act of 1964, other existing or proposed legislation may help the small library. Laws relating to control or prevention of juvenile delinquency or extension of economic opportunity may, for example, enable the library to employ young people as library helpers with the federal government paying a substantial share of their salaries. While not all these laws will be administered by the state library agency, the state staff will be acquainted with the possibilities and able to give information and advice. Other excellent sources of information about federal legislation are the *ALA Washington Newsletter,* the regular "Washington Report" in the *ALA Bulletin,* and the frequent summaries of federal library-related legislation in other library periodicals.

Governmental and Professional Relationships

While the library usually operates under a special law and may have an administrative structure differing from that of other local services, it is still very much a part of local government. Like other public agencies, it is supported primarily by local taxes. To a greater or less degree, it follows the local pattern in such matters as financial accountability, personnel procedure, purchasing, and budget presentation. Local conditions will vary, and it is important that the trustees and librarian know their particular situation well.

Where there is a good, businesslike local government structure, it is to the advantage of the library to avail itself of the knowledge and skill of local officials. For example, the purchasing officer may have made comparative studies of adding machines that will be useful to the library, or the finance officer may be able to give the staff member in charge of the library's bookkeeping suggestions for keeping the accounts more effectively. A cordial working relationship should be maintained in the many matters in which the library's business brings board or librarian in contact with other officials.

In addition to its close relationship with local government, the library also has relationships with the state, with other libraries, and with library associations. Although the local librarian may be the only library administrator in his own community, he is not alone; he is part of a profession, and his library is part of a statewide, even a national, network of libraries with similar programs and goals. All these affiliations are valuable and should be utilized to make the local library a better one.

A most important relationship, both professional and legal in some states, is that of the library with the state library agency. The functions, policies, and resources of state agencies vary, but in every state the local librarian can turn to his state library for help of many kinds. State consultants are familiar with statewide library practices and problems. Part of their job is to keep up to date on professional matters to an extent that the local librarian usually cannot equal. At the same time they are familiar enough with the realities of the small library's situation to give sound and practical advice about adapting locally to new trends. A state consultant's services are not, as some librarians mistakenly believe, useful only to untrained librarians. To request and use all the help the state consultant can give is an indication of competence, not a sign of weakness. The state agency, in its turn, often calls on local librarians for cooperation: in assisting at a workshop or in writing up successful programs or innovations for the state library's newsletter.

State library consultants assist the local library in various ways: by letters of professional advice, with bibliographies of recent professional literature on a requested topic, through visits and on-the-spot counsel, and by attending meetings of boards, officials, or Friends of the Library. Professional books and periodicals, building plans and slides, and sample budgets and policies are usually available on loan from the state library, as are also specialized books not found in the local collection and, in some states, general rotating book collections. Most state libraries fill requests for specific books or subject material. Some operate union catalogs; some offer processing service at a reasonable cost. Almost every state agency publishes important library statistics and issues a newsletter or journal containing useful information. Workshops and institutes offered at the state level are usually of great practical value to the librarians who attend.

State libraries are often called extension agencies, because one of their functions is to assist in extending library service throughout the state. In another sense, they may be thought of as extensions of the local library's resources. The local library is entitled, by virtue of the support given by local taxpayers to the state budget, to receive whatever services are offered by the state agency. Librarians should make use of this valuable resource to improve local library service.

Professional assistance may also be obtained from library organizations: state, regional, and national. These resources, too, should be fully used. State associations vary greatly in strength, but in most areas either a state or a regional association makes studies, provides guidance, and offers special services through committees. The state association usually spearheads new legislation or the repeal of frustrating, obsolete laws. Problems involving intellectual freedom are also of concern to state associations, and assistance in dealing with such problems is usually available if needed. Through publications and meetings, state and regional associations provide also the opportunity for valuable exchange of information among librarians on questions of professional concern.

The American Library Association offers many kinds of help and maintains at its headquarters a variety of aids that may be borrowed, such as building plans and slides. The local library benefits much from institutional membership in the American Library Association, as well as through individual staff and trustee memberships. Among the many advantages the American Library Association offers to the profession are its publications, its studies, its advisory services, and the invaluable assistance given by its Washington office in protecting the interests of libraries in such national matters as postal rates, surplus property distribution, and federal grants to states for library service.

Working with Trustees

The most important of the librarian's official relationships is that with his board of trustees. Dealing with such a body is apt to be a new experience for the beginning library administrator. While individual boards vary considerably and state and local laws differ, some aspects of the trustee relationship are common to most library situations.

Broadly speaking, the librarian represents the profession and the trustees the community. The librarian brings to his job special training, knowledge, and skill which are not shared by a lay board. The role of the trustees is to set policy suited to the community served, to try to obtain the best librarian and library service it can afford, and to interpret the library's functions, needs, and objectives to the community.

Selecting a librarian is one of the board's chief obligations. It should obtain the services of a capable one in whom it has confidence and to whom it can safely entrust the administration of the library. Having done so, it should leave the responsibility for actual operation of the library to the librarian and support him fully as long as he follows the policies agreed upon. For example, while the board will concern itself with staff salaries and pensions, it will not become involved with assignment of specific library tasks. In consultation with the librarian, the board will plan for library development and determine broad policy in matters such as the selection of library materials, but it will leave to the professional judgment of the librarian the choice of the actual books in the collection.

The trustees, in representing the community, are not representing the taxpayer in the narrow sense. Their chief responsibility is not to keep library expenditures to a minimum, but rather to make sure that the community has the best library service it can reasonably be expected to pay for. Library boards are also responsible for approving and presenting the budget and for library buildings and other property.

Before establishing policies, the board has an obligation to become acquainted with good library practice. The librarian himself is the chief source of information and will often prepare drafts of policy statements for board approval. Furthermore, the good librarian will welcome and stimulate the desire of his trustees to learn more about libraries in general, to visit other libraries, to read professional literature, and especially to join national and state associations and attend their meetings.

The librarian-trustee relationship is close and, ideally, harmonious. It should also be businesslike. In a small community, the librarian, board members, library staff, and their families may enjoy social friendships. If these relationships are allowed to filter into board meetings—or, even worse, if the habit develops of staff discussion of everyday library matters with a friendly trustee—a serious breakdown of authority can result.

When librarian and trustees cooperate for the development of the library and agree on fundamental objectives and principles, board meetings can be most satisfying experiences. Such agreement and harmony are well worth patient effort and open-minded discussion by all. In his trustees the librarian is fortunate to have a community group that is required to take an interest in the library and to meet regularly to discuss its affairs. If he is a newcomer who has many changes in mind, he may make the mistake of trying to move too fast. If he sees the trustees as an obstacle rather than as an opportunity, if he is impatient of what seems to him their slowness to accept his plans, if he attempts to coerce them into acceptance or even to act without their approval in matters they should know about, and especially if he fails to realize their value as touchstones of community opinion, he will more often impede than advance library development. A good librarian who knows his job can win the confidence of his trustees and finds, in turn, that he can have confidence in them—assuming, of course, that the board is made up of people who have a concern for the good of their community and an interest in education and reading, or at least the potential for developing such interest and concern.

While the ideal board of trustees takes an interest in the library, supports the librarian, and leaves the administration to him, actual trustees may have developed habits, perhaps because of relationships with previous librarians, that vary from this ideal. A board that goes rapidly through routine business to get the meetings over as soon as possible may not have been taken into the confidence of a former librarian. Such a board needs the stimulus of lively reports and participation in policy discussions in order to be encouraged toward constructive activity. On the other hand, if the previous librarian has been passive, timid, or inept in some aspects of administration, the trustees may perforce have had to assume some functions that should belong to the professional administrator. This situation is not an easy one for a newcomer, but changes in the relationship can be successfully effected by an able librarian and civic-minded trustees without loss of good will on either side.

The Role of Trustees in a Library System

If the library is considering system membership, one of the questions that frequently causes concern is the role of the board. A good group of trustees that have served their community well and grown interested in the future of the library will naturally want to continue to share in library affairs. Board members will want to know their status when and if the library affiliates with a larger unit.[1]

There is no one standard relationship between trustees of local libraries and the administering agencies of library systems. The organization of systems is still developing; new patterns are being worked out. Boards may feel sure, however, that no matter what structure emerges, the library urgently needs citi-

---

[1] For examples of actual situations in which local boards operate within library systems, see the footnote on page 7.

zens who feel a deep concern about their library service at the local level. Librarians working toward better library service through systems recognize the importance of utilizing the interest and knowledge of these lay groups.

What the new role of the board will be depends on the type of system. The functions of the trustees may be enlarged in some areas and lessened in others. If the library becomes the agency through which an expanded service is given to a larger area, new funds will be available and new responsibilities undertaken. In such a case, librarian and board alike may be accountable to another, perhaps an additional, jurisdiction. If, for example, the local library extends its service through contract to the surrounding county area, the board will negotiate with county officials for funds and consult with local county groups on the best methods of reaching county readers.

In the cooperative type of system, the board's function may change very little. It will continue to operate in its own library as it has in the past, except for functions now performed on a system-wide basis. For example, a system of local libraries may plan a film service for all its members and a processing center serving the whole system. These two functions may be carried on by two different member libraries. The board of the library giving system-wide film service will take on new responsibilities; there will be new types of expenditure for films and equipment and new staff. On the other hand, that particular board will no longer be concerned with processing for its own library, since that work will be assigned to another system member. Of course, all the librarians and boards will have been involved in the original planning for the sharing of the new services and the financing of them.

In another type of cooperative system, system-wide services are set up separately under a newly formed system board, usually made up of representatives of the local boards of member libraries. The new governing body works with the librarians concerned to employ personnel, set policies, obtain space, and generally act as trustees for the entire membership in connection with the services for which it is responsible.

If a library becomes part of a more centralized system, its local board may continue to serve as an advisory council, helping at first to smooth the details of the transition (which it itself has brought about) and interpreting the new arrangement to the community. Later this type of advisory council assists the central administration by advising about local needs and conditions and continuing to interpret the service to the local community.

Working without a Board

The degree to which boards control the policies of their libraries varies considerably. In some libraries, the board acts with almost complete independence of other governmental officials. Increasingly, however, this picture seems to be changing, as new laws and regulations tend to increase the area of control of professional public administrators. For example, a new civil service law may apply to the library as well as to other local agencies and may automatically abridge the board's jurisdiction in personnel matters. Purchasing is another area in which centralized control is apt to be established, and the library may be required to channel its purchases through a central office.[2]

Where there is a city manager, there is a tendency, in particular, to abolish lay boards or to change their role to an advisory one. The manager works directly with the various department heads, of whom the librarian is one. In some ways the librarian has more independence, in others, less. The manager will perhaps inquire very little into the library's service, for example, but will ask many searching questions about the financial and business operations. The change requires an adjustment for the librarian, who may miss the support of his citizen board. Having more direct access to the central organs of local government, he will automatically be brought into closer contact with other officials. He will be called upon, within the usually limited time the manager is able to devote to the library, to give many explanations of the library's functions, operations, and needs. Normally, he will present and justify the library's budget to the manager or to the taxing body himself rather than relying on the board of trustees as an intermediary. There is no reason why the librarian who works directly with a city manager should not develop a satisfactory relationship. As with a new board, time and patience may be needed to achieve the mutual understanding that makes for good teamwork. As a department head

[2] See p.56–58 for a discussion of the library's relationship with a personnel officer and p.141–42 for its relationship with a purchasing department.

working under a manager, the librarian becomes a full-fledged member of the official family, not set apart by a special status that makes him an exception. He attends department-head meetings called by the manager. His contacts with his official colleagues become a part of normal procedure, no longer requiring a special effort on his part. He is in touch, regularly, with the whole of community government; knows all official community affairs; and has constant opportunities to present the library's functions and services to his colleagues and to learn, in turn, how the library can serve their needs. His regular contacts with budgeting, purchasing, accounting, and personnel officials will help him in understanding and dealing with these departments, and may also give the library ready access to their facilities and staff help. He may well find, therefore, that his department-head status stands him in good stead at budget time and on many other occasions throughout the year.

Friends of the Library

For libraries without trustees, and for others as well, the organization of a group of Friends of the Library provides a valuable contact with citizen library users. Ideally and theoretically, such a group of Friends organizes spontaneously; realistically, the library administration may have to start the group. Unless a citizen has been active elsewhere in a Friends of the Library organization, there is usually no local knowledge of the possibilities for action by such a group until the librarian explains them.

The role and activities of Friends of the Library vary widely. Theirs is not an advisory function, and it is a mistake to allow such a body to act as an unofficial board, studying library operations, making recommendations, and the like. Occasionally an aggressive community leader, active in the Friends group, will attempt to move into spheres that are properly those of the librarian and trustees; such attempts, even if prompted by genuine interest and helpfulness, are fraught with potential problems and must be discouraged. The Friends can usually be encouraged to write into their bylaws a statement of purpose that includes appropriate objectives, such as sponsoring public programs, undertaking fund-raising activities that may result in substantial gifts to the library, and assisting with community study and public relations work. The very existence of a group of

Friends, with no motive except a wish to help the library because it believes in the library, is impressive to the community and to officials alike.

The librarian who wishes to encourage the formation of a group of Friends of the Library will want, first, to gather information about the organization and activities of groups elsewhere. The state library agency, the Library Trustees Association of the American Library Association or of his own state, and articles in the professional journals are all good sources to which to turn for material. From this information the librarian will select what seems locally appropriate and call it to the attention of one or more active community leaders already interested in the library. Every librarian has at his fingertips the names of friends of the library who need only a little encouragement to become organized Friends. Whether he begins with one person or calls together a small group to discuss the idea will depend on the local situation. A natural leader whom everyone likes may be the best person to approach, but it is a mistake to start with someone who may become possessive or overaggressive.

The librarian's role during the organization of a Friends group is a delicate one. He wishes to develop a relationship that will assure an autonomous group capable of speaking independently for the library if necessary, but one that will also consult him about the kinds of help and gifts the library needs. The printed information he makes available to the organizers will help, and he can set the right tone in his first approach to the prospective leaders. He should not take the lead in the actual meetings for the purpose of organizing the group, but should be available to give information that will help start it in the right direction.

The Budget

The most important part of library business in which the librarian and board work together is the preparation of the budget. A budget, like much else in library management, is made easier by careful planning. The year's budget might be considered a program for the coming year's activities with price tags attached to the various items. If librarian and trustees are agreed on objectives and have worked out together a long-range plan for library development, preparation of a budget becomes a matter of determining how much of the program can be attempted in any particular year in the light of current costs and local financial conditions. If the long-range plan has been approved in principle by the appropriating or taxing body or by planning officials, as well as by the library board, preparing the budget and securing approval become even simpler.

Long-range budget planning is one of the library administrator's most important duties. It is only too easy, under pressure of everyday tasks, to operate on a year-to-year basis, taking advantage of opportunities when they arise and tightening the library belt when conditions are unfavorable. But many librarians and boards have found that a careful, detailed, and imaginative plan for better library service, with clearly indicated stages for implementation from year to year, will be favorably received by both the community at large and by officials. Such a plan should take into account whatever information is available from local and state sources as to population projections and movements; community advances in educational and other facilities; any proposed major highways, thoroughfares, or industries; and potential revenue from state and federal sources. Where cooperative or system developments are anticipated, their implications, too, should be considered in the long-range plan. It is not usually possible to budget in detail on a long-range basis, but it is wise to estimate costs and to take into account in such an estimate the probable increases in salaries and the prices of major items involved.

Most libraries operate on a "line"-type budget, which indicates how much is available for salaries, how much for equipment, and so on. This type of budget can be extremely detailed or somewhat general. It may, for example, list each position and the exact salary attached to it or may indicate only a lump sum for all salaries. Similarly, it may allocate a sum for total equipment, or it may specify so much for a typewriter, so much for a book truck, and so forth. Preparing a detailed budget and operating under it require care and foresight—one reason why many public administrators favor such budgets. The divisions usually found in a line-type budget are Salaries, Capital Outlay, and Operating Expenditures, although the exact terms used may vary. For the library, the first item covers actual salaries and retirement contributions; Capital Outlay includes major expenditures such as construction, remodeling, or a bookmobile, plus furniture and equipment costing above a predetermined sum; Operating Expenditures includes supplies, utilities, insurance, services, repairs, along with minor items of equipment or furniture, such as wastebaskets.

Since the three categories of the average budget are set up for all functions of the total government unit, they do not make special provision for one of the library's major budget items—books and other library materials. Some libraries simply add a section to the budget to cover materials; others must include them within the broader budget structure. Libraries are sometimes faced with a serious problem when books are budgeted in the Capital Outlay section. Local regulations in many communities require competitive bidding before a capital item can be bought, as well as special marks of ownership and regular inventories of capital purchases. While the book collection as a whole is the library's most important possession and represents a long-term public investment, individual books are lost and withdrawn almost every day. Cumbersome procurement and accountability procedures are not feasible for a possession so fluid, and many libraries have found it advisable to include the book budget under Operating Expenditures. If local regulations make it impossible to remove books from the Capital Outlay section of the budget, the librarian should discuss with the appropriate officials methods of simplifying procedures as much as possible to meet the library's special needs.[3]

Of late years the performance budget has been increasingly used. Its purpose is to break down expenditures so that the budget reflects the total cost of each major part of the library program. The procedures used in arriving at figures for such a budget might be compared with the accounting methods by which department stores judge the success of a given department. To the candy counter, for example, are charged overhead, rent according to its location, salaries, advertising, and other operating costs, as well as the cost of the merchandise itself. The income from sales is evaluated in relation to these costs. Similarly, in a library the cost of a particular service might be determined; for example, cataloging costs would include personnel (including a share of administration, if administration is not included separately), supplies, equipment, overhead, and so on. The total figure, divided by the number of books to be cataloged, would give a unit cost of cataloging per book.

[3] See "Acquisition of Materials," p.136–39, and "Inventory," p.149.

The value of the performance method is that it gives an objective measure against which to assess needs. If a library expects to add so many more books next year, and if costs of salaries and supplies have increased at a known rate, one can readily see that the money needed to prepare the new books will come to a specific figure. Certain problems are created for the library by this method, however. The initial assessment of costs is of obvious importance, yet it is extremely difficult to calculate, especially in the case of operations performed by several people at odd moments. Work taken home and done on the staff's own time also distorts the picture. Another difficulty is that, if the library's performance is not up to standard, the unit cost will reflect such substandard service, and budget increases may be obtainable only for increased workloads. Under the performance method, it is easier to get more money for more work than it is to get it for better work.

While it is not suggested that the average small library will want to adopt a performance budget, the librarian should know the principles, some of which will be helpful in his own budget plans. When he thinks in terms of the cost of each operation, he becomes aware of the relative costs of the different segments of the library's service and can ask whether the proportions seem justified. As an example, suppose a small library is considering adding bookmobile service. In a line budget, the cost of the bookmobile itself—its generator, heater, air conditioner, and so on—are listed under Capital Outlay, its staff under Salaries, its books included in the total for library materials. Under Operating Expenditures are included such items as gas, oil, servicing, and repairs. In a performance budget the cost of the equipment, staff, books, and upkeep would be gathered under one heading to show just how much the bookmobile service would cost. A librarian accustomed to thinking of total costs is aware of the costs of preparing new books and the costs attendant on an expected increase in circulation: reserves, overdues, and the like. He can thus decide whether the new service is justified in its relationship to the overall budget of the library.

Even when there is no plan for a new service, performance-budget thinking is helpful. A simple example, applicable to every library, can be found in the cost of maintaining the book collection at its current strength. Such a figure would include books to replace the normal percentage of losses and withdrawals, renewal of periodical subscriptions, other replacements such as pamphlets and documents, film circuit membership if any, *and* the staff and supply costs involved in withdrawing discarded materials and acquiring and preparing the replacements. It is often a surprise to officials—and sometimes to librarians and board members—to learn how much of the budget is necessary even to hold the line in the library's collection.

Whatever the type of budget, the philosophy behind the performance budget is close to that the librarian and trustees will actually adopt. They determine what they hope to accomplish during the coming year, then consider how much the program will cost. The library does not only ask for this sum; it must explain what it expects to do with the money, why the program is worth doing, how it fits into the total library picture and the community's needs, and sometimes quite specifically why a particular item is superior to various alternatives.

A justification for a request for an additional book truck, for example, might read like this:

This item of equipment is needed to speed up the shelving of books returned by readers. At the present time, the library employs two part-time pages who shelve books after school, instead of one full-time page as formerly. Each must have a truck at the same time. Other available trucks are in use, one to receive new books as they are processed, one to receive returned books at the loan desk. Removing books from either of these trucks to allow for its use by the shelving page is time-consuming and disrupts library operations at other points.

A request for more money for children's books might cite an increase in juvenile population or in juvenile library use, the heavy wear and tear on children's books (with figures for replacement or rebinding), increases in the costs of books (also with figures). The need to replace juvenile encyclopedias, the number of requests unmet because of insufficient book stock, the proportion of the collection out in circulation, and the resulting paucity of books available to those coming to the library might also be mentioned. Whatever the justification, it should be as specific as possible, clearly stated, accurate, and able to withstand investigation.

Budget justifications will often include mention of increased circulation. Circulation figures are the time-honored measures of a library's effectiveness. Although librarians know that such statistics offer only a partial yardstick for measurement of accomplishment, they continue to use them for want of a better one. However, the librarian who, under the stimulus of growing library use, makes his plea for a larger budget solely on the basis of circulation increases, may be asking for trouble later. Should circulation level off, he may still legitimately need an increased budget, but he has not laid any groundwork for requesting one. The library may have been operating almost as a book cafeteria during a period of rapid growth, with scarcely any reference service, community activity, or reader guidance possible because of the greatly increased circulation. Its service to the individual reader may be inferior to that given before the boom period. The librarian must think ahead to future budget requests and if the library is currently, for all its expansion, failing to hold the line or barely managing to do so, make this clear to officials.

In addition to the written justification, most library budgets are granted a hearing before a budget official or appropriating body. Such a hearing offers an invaluable opportunity to explain the library's function and needs. Often the board president takes the lead in presenting the budget, with the librarian available to answer questions. Whatever the circumstances, this important interview is usually brief. It behooves the person representing the library to be sure of his facts and to make the most of the short time available.

If the budget calls for a greatly expanded program for a library that has heretofore filled a modest role, a special effort in budget presentation is necessary. Such an effort should include:

> Prior acceptance of a long-range plan by officials, if this can be arranged, so that the budget is recognized as the first step toward agreed-upon improvements
>
> Full and freely expressed board approval and support of the program
>
> Evidence of citizen support, expressed either by written endorsements or by the presence and possibly testimony of community leaders. For example, if the P.T.A. has helped with the community survey that has led to the submission of the new budget, it would be helpful if that organization were to present a resolution. The value of a large attendance at the budget hearing will depend on the normal extent of community participation in such hearings. Some officials react negatively to what appears

to them to be an attempt to influence their judgment by
pressure

Brief and clear-cut justifications and explanations, with meaningful comparisons and statistics from the experiences of
other libraries

Realistic but not overmodest appraisal of the library's needs
in relation to the total budget of the community

Working within a Budget

Once a budget has been approved, the librarian must plan
his year's operation on the basis of the funds he has been allowed. If he is fortunate enough to have obtained what he
requested, his planning is probably already done. If he has been
granted only enough to continue service as formerly given, he
may have little planning to do. If, however, he has been allotted
some, but not all, of the increase he requested, he may have to
make a choice. Sometimes a librarian has little or nothing to
say about the disposition of a budget increase. The items allowed
or disallowed by officials are specific, and he must abide by the
decision. In other cases, he may have some leeway in deciding
how to use the additional funds: which of two requested assistants is more important, for example, or whether the children's
replacements are more urgently needed than the new reference
books. Probably in both cases he will consider a compromise,
buying some children's and some reference books and adding one
new person who can do part of the needed work.

No matter how disappointing the appropriation, the librarian
must try to accept it with good grace and fit his program to his
library income. The dramatic gesture to highlight the library's
need—by curtailing hours or spending the entire book fund
during the first six months—is seldom wise. It is true that on occasion such an action will rally public support, but it can back-
fire. Even if it is successful one time, it can lead to problems with
budget officials in future years. Of course, if the librarian and
board, in presenting the budget, have warned that hours will
have to be curtailed unless sufficient salary money is appropriated, they must follow through; otherwise their justifications will
cease to be taken seriously. Such warnings, however, should not
be made unless the librarian and board will carry them out.

In every library, and especially in the smaller one, an
emergency situation may warrant a request for a supplementary
appropriation. A prolonged illness during which a senior staff

member's salary must be paid, for example, will use up the part-time and substitute salary money early in the budget year. In such a case, a special request is necessary, and it is usually easy to show that the library must have extra funds to carry on without a serious curtailment of service. Most jurisdictions carry contingency funds for such emergencies.

In spending the monies allotted to the library, the librarian will follow prescribed procedures as to payroll, warrants, and bookkeeping. Even if the library board is in complete control of expenditures, signs its own checks, and arranges for its own audit, it is advisable to tailor the library's business methods to those followed by other departments, insofar as is feasible for the library operation. Official confidence in the way in which library funds are spent and accounted for is an asset well-worth striving to attain.

Financial Accountability

As a public official, the librarian is responsible for the expenditure and safeguarding of public money. The funds entrusted to him should be spent as wisely as possible, the records be in order, and all money accounted for. Any appearance of laxity should be scrupulously avoided; such practices as staff borrowing from the fine money, for example, must not be permitted.

For small, everyday expenditures, it is helpful to have a petty cash fund that may be used by the librarian as needed. Occasional emergencies arise in which small items such as display materials or paperbacks may be needed in a hurry, for which a cash purchase is necessary. When petty cash is used, a receipt should be obtained if possible; in any case, a record should be kept of the expenditure, with date, purpose, and supplier. The petty cash fund is usually kept small and replenished when it runs low, to avoid its use for items that could be ordered and billed in the regular way.

Cash receipts should be counted daily and kept in a safe place until they can be deposited. Postage stamps and supplies should be safeguarded, with only enough for normal current needs immediately accessible to all. While such a careful policy may seem overstrict to the staff, and even a reflection on its honesty, it is in reality a protection. Waste, carelessness, or personal use of publicly owned property, however minor, can

34

create a most unfortunate impression with the public. The wise librarian leans over backward to avoid even the appearance of such practices.

Fines and Fees

Most public libraries have some income as well as expenditures, and money taken in over the desk should be recorded as carefully as appropriated or tax funds. What kinds of fines and fees, and how high they will be, are questions to be determined by the trustees after consultation with the librarian.

The charging of fines for overdue books is so much an accepted part of library methodology that it is usually taken for granted. A few libraries however, have reported successful results in charging no fines at all. Librarians who believe in the no-fine philosophy contend that readers who want to keep books overdue feel completely within their rights so long as they are willing to pay the necessary fines, but develop a sense of obligation to return books on time when there is no penalty.

Librarians and officials are not in agreement as to the chief purpose of fines. Is it to assure the prompt return of books, to penalize thoughtless and selfish users, to provide revenue, or to defray the costs of overdue procedures? Most librarians would concur in the opinion that the prompt return of books is the major objective; if this is true, the system of fines should be judged primarily on the basis of its effectiveness in bringing books back to the library on time. In some libraries, the policy of fines may actually prevent the return of books and may cut down the use of the library. "Forgiveness days" as practiced in a number of communities show that many people are afraid to return library books that are long overdue. Newspaper stories occasionally tell of books returned after many years, and reporters seem to take pleasure in computing the astronomical fines that have accrued. Readers of the stories do not always know that the maximum fine of most libraries is fairly modest.

Whether to charge fines, how much, whether to differentiate in the case of children, are decisions that should be made on the basis of experience in a particular community; like other library decisions, they should be made deliberately and not by default.

Even libraries that have eliminated fines expect readers to pay for lost books. It is wise to have a clear-cut policy on what the amount to be paid is based. The loser of a book is naturally hopeful that such factors will be taken into account as the age and condition of the book, depreciation, the existence of cheap reprints, and special circumstances of the loss or damage which he feels lessen his own responsibility. He is not usually aware of factors the library must bear in mind, such as cost of replacement, increase in list price, cost of acquisition and processing, and the possibility that the book may be out-of-print. Some readers suppose that libraries can buy books at fantastically low discounts or even get them free from publishers automatically.

Most public libraries, when charging replacement cost for lost books, use the list price rather than the discount price to compensate in some measure for costs of processing. Book losses due to such misfortunes as fires and floods are usually written off. Common sense also rules out such rigid practices as charging fines and book costs to the estates of deceased readers.

It is most important that all readers should be treated alike in any action of the library involving money. Nothing creates more indignation than the suspicion that favoritism has been shown to some, or that a strict interpretation of a rule by one staff member might have been eased by another. It follows, therefore, that the rules should be written out, in order that they can be applied consistently.

Another type of charge is the fee for library use by nonresidents. Current trends, at first glance apparently contradictory, are to increase such fees on the one hand and to eliminate them on the other.

Increases in charges to nonresident borrowers reflect the concern of officials and taxpayers alike at the rising cost of government service. If there is no nonresident fee, or if the fee is lower than the average cost per borrower of the library operation, then it is obvious that the nonresident is being favored and that local taxpayers are paying for all or part of the service the nonresidents receive. When officials become aware of this disparity, they logically wish to charge a higher fee. Librarians, whose natural instincts are to encourage reading and library use, sometimes are reluctant to raise the fee, realizing it may even turn away some borrowers of long standing. In the long run, however, it is probably not in the best interest of future library service to give all comers, taxpayers or not, equal library privileges. When a local library generously assumes a function that should be a neighboring community's responsibility, the neighboring community has little spur to meet its own obligation.

There is also a trend in the opposite direction—toward elimination of nonresident fees. This trend reflects two developments. First, it is being recognized that the nonresident fee for borrowing privileges does not really compensate a library for use by nonresidents. Free use of reference materials by nonresidents and free telephone information service may cost the library at least as much as the privilege of borrowing books. Yet nonresident use of these services can scarcely be charged for on an individual basis. Libraries heavily used in these ways by nonresidents are beginning to feel the pinch and are entitled to some compensation. The second development, the tendency toward contract services, interlibrary cooperation, or both, makes possible the equitable abolition of nonresident fees in a number of ways. Neighboring small libraries with fairly equal resources can give reciprocal service freely to readers from both communities. Small libraries can contract with larger ones to enable residents of the smaller community to use the larger library; communities without libraries can pay a neighboring library to expand its service to their residents. In some states, state or federal funds are paid to large libraries to serve as resource centers for an entire state or area without direct cost to the individual borrower.

When the question of an increased nonresident fee is considered, therefore, the librarian may wish to propose an alternative. It may well be that the best interests of library service in his own community lie not in tightening restrictions and raising the fee, but in a cooperative arrangement with a neighboring community.

Insurance

Whether to insure the library building and its contents, what type of insurance to obtain, and what proportion of the appraised value to cover by insurance are questions to be considered by the trustees or other governing body responsible for library property. Control may reside in the city or county or with the board. In some situations the building is the responsibility of the larger authority, the books that of the trustees.

The librarian's responsibilities are twofold. First, he must know what protection exists and be familiar with the official philosophy governing the existing coverage. If the present coverage seems out of line with the philosophy—for example, if a policy that gave full coverage years ago has not been increased—

it is his obligation to call the disparity to the attention of the proper officials. His second responsibility results from the fact that he alone is in a position adequately to estimate the value of the book collection and such important properties as the catalog and shelf list—values not always understood by appraisers and officials. He must therefore be prepared to assist appraisers in making a just valuation.

Boards and other governing bodies have varying reactions to the possibility of loss or damage. Some feel that the risks are slight and therefore carry no insurance, preferring to risk the loss and save the premiums. Large jurisdictions with many scattered properties also often carry no insurance, on the theory that the cost of relatively large premiums over a period of years would be greater than the necessary replacements and repairs in the event of damage. Such large jurisdictions are usually financially better able to stand losses than a small community. If a serious fire or flood would damage the library so badly that the financial burden of resuming service would be severe or impossible, then some type of protection is needed.

Self-insurance—that is, the setting aside of a regular sum to cover possible loss and damage over a period of years—is another method of protection frequently found. Many jurisdictions carry some insurance temporarily while such a fund is being built up. If self-insurance is the method used locally, the fund carried to protect property should be kept for that purpose and not be drawn on for other needs. In other words, it should not be looked on as a general contingency fund.

If the library carries insurance, the librarian must determine, in the light of the total library program and the time available, how careful an appraisal of the value of the book collection and shelf list he can afford to make. If there is a special collection of considerable value, it should be evaluated separately, perhaps by a professional book appraiser or dealer; otherwise, the library could not recover its full value in case of loss. Assistance in estimating the monetary value of the basic collection is available in the records of average cost per volume or other category issued periodically by the Insurance for Libraries Committee of the Library Administration Division of the American Library Association; the *Bowker Annual of Library and Book Trade Information;* and the Annual Summary issue of *Publishers' Weekly* (the third issue in January). A listing of average costs for the current year (1964), derived from these sources, is given on pages 38–39.

AVERAGE COSTS OF A BASIC COLLECTION

Adult fiction	$ 4.15
Juveniles	3.10
Adult nonfiction	
Art	10.70
Biography	6.75
Business	9.75
Economics	7.65
Education	5.50
History	7.75
Literature	4.50
Medicine	11.25
Music	7.00
Religion	4.65
Science	11.00
Sports	6.15
Technology	11.00
Periodicals	
Business and Economics	6.26
Chemistry and Physics	16.50
Education	5.00
Engineering	7.32
Fine Arts	15.00
General	5.85
History and English	10.00
Law	11.00
Library Science	5.01
Music	10.00
Political Science	5.33
Sociology and Anthropology	5.07
Documents	
Paper bulletins	.31
Paperbound volumes	1.90
Bound volumes	4.00
Periodical volumes	4.00
Music (no figures available for scores because of the diversity of materials)	
Sheet	.60
Maps	1.00

Microreproductions
    Microfilm (per reel)   5.25
    Microprint (per card)   .40
    Microcard (per card)   .25
Audio-visual materials
    Films—silent
        16 mm. black and white (per reel)   30.00
        16 mm. color (per reel)   55.00
    Film—sound
        16 mm. black and white (per reel)   68.00
        16 mm. color (per reel)   115.00
Filmstrip
    Black and white (per unit)   3.00
    Color (per unit)   5.00
Slides
    Black and white (2 × 2)   .30
    Color (2 × 2)   .50
Phonograph records—33⅓ rpm
    10″ disc   3.00
    12″ disc   4.00
Stereophonic records   4.75
Tapes   12.00

The library discount and depreciation[4] would need to be computed before applying these costs in ascertaining the value of a collection.

While library management will inevitably take a large proportion of the beginning administrator's time and will always remain an important activity, it must not absorb all his attention. He can save time for service and for building the collection by mastering the techniques and information necessary for good administration and by delegating as many administrative details as possible.

[4] Depreciation figures by category are given in American Library Association, Library Technology Project, *Protecting the Library and Its Resources: A Guide to Physical Protection and Insurance* (Chicago: A.L.A., 1963), p.263.

Bibliography

American Library Association. Library Administration Division. Friends of Libraries Committee. *Friends of the Library: Organization and Activities,* ed. by Sarah Leslie Wallace. Chicago: A.L.A., 1962. 111p.

———— Public Libraries Division. *Contracts and Agreements for Public Library Service,* comp. by Lura G. Currier. (PLD Reporter, no.6) Chicago: A.L.A., 1958. 58p.

———— ———— *Friends of Public Libraries: How They Work.* (PLD Reporter, no.3) Chicago: A.L.A., 1955. 73p.

———— Public Library Association. *Public Library Policies—General and Specific.* (Public Library Reporter, no.9) Chicago: A.L.A., 1960. 109p.

Bowler, Roberta, ed. *Local Public Library Administration.* Chicago: International City Managers' Assn., 1964. 375p.

Eggen, J. Archer, ed. "Library Boards," *Library Trends,* 11:3–93 (July, 1962).

Gallagher, Marian G. "Internal Administration and Its Organization," *Library Trends,* 6:399–411 (April, 1958).

Hamill, Harold L. "Executive-Board Relations in Public Libraries," *Library Trends,* 7:388–97 (January, 1959).

Long, Norton E. "The Public Librarian's Boss," in J. Periam Danton, ed., *The Climate of Book Selection,* p.27–34. Berkeley: Univ. of California School of Librarianship, 1959.

Munn, R. Russell. "Present-Day Public Library Executives," *Library Trends,* 7:398–406 (January, 1959).

Wheeler, Joseph L., and Goldhor, Herbert. *Practical Administration of Public Libraries.* New York: Harper, 1962. 571p.

Young, Virginia, ed. *The Library Trustee: A Practical Guidebook.* New York: Bowker, 1964. 184p.

———— *The Trustee of a Small Public Library.* (Small Libraries Project Pamphlet, no.3) Chicago: A.L.A., 1962. 15p.

Budget and Finance

American Library Association. Public Library Association. *Costs of Public Library Service, 1963.* Chicago: A.L.A., 1964. 18p.

Baldwin, Emma V., and Marcus, William E. *Library Costs and Budgets: A Study of Cost Accounting in Public Libraries.* New York: Bowker, 1941. 201p. Somewhat out-of-date, but still useful, as are also the titles by Bray and Wight, following.

Bray, Helen E. *The Library's Financial Records.* New York: Bowker, 1943. 58p.

Higgins, Charles L. "Budgeting for Library Service," *Bookmark* (New York State Library), 23:155–59 (March, 1964).

Maybury, Catherine. "Performance Budgeting for the Library," *ALA Bulletin,* 55:46–53 (January, 1961).

"Missouri Library Experiments with No Fines for Overdues," *Library Journal,* 87:2111 (June 1, 1962).

Parker, R. H., and Price, Paxton, eds. "Aspects of the Financial Administration of Libraries," *Library Trends,* 11:341–451 (April, 1963).

Peterson, Harry N. "Performance Budgeting, Work Measurement, and the Public Library," *Wilson Library Bulletin,* 27:620–23 (April, 1953).

Stevens, Harris. "How to Build a Library Budget," *Library Journal,* 82:2067–72 (September 15, 1957).

Ten Haken, Richard E. "Securing Library Support," *Bookmark* (New York State Library), 23:159–62 (March, 1964).

Wight, Edward A. *Public Library Finance and Accounting.* Chicago: A.L.A., 1943. 137p.

Insurance

American Library Association. Library Technology Project. *Protecting the Library and Its Resources: A Guide to Physical Protection and Insurance.* (LTP Publications, no.7) Chicago: A.L.A., 1963. 322p.

Hemphill, B. F. "Lessons of a Fire," *Library Journal,* 87:1094–95 (March 15, 1962).

Singer, Dorothea M. *The Insurance of Libraries: A Manual for Librarians.* Chicago: A.L.A., 1946. 92p.

3

PERSONNEL ADMINISTRATION

If a decision had to be made as to whether a good book collection or a good staff was more important to a library, a strong case could be made for the primary importance of staff. Without at least one person qualified to select books, a good collection could not long remain good, and certainly a good collection would to some extent be wasted without a staff that could organize it for service and help readers use it to best advantage. Moreover, a competent staff is able to utilize to the fullest even a small collection and to strengthen it by careful selection and weeding. Another measure of the importance of personnel is the proportion of the library's budget that is earmarked for salaries. Approximately 65 percent is the normal and irreducible allotment for personnel if the library is to prepare and service its book collection adequately.

In view of this proportion, the library administrator can hardly be unmindful of his responsibilities for personnel administration. Naturally, the small public library will have a small staff—a situation that raises its own special problems. It is scarcely necessary to point out that a small staff needs to be selected with at least as much care as the larger staff of a larger library. In fact, a poor staff member in a small group is more of a problem than a poor staff member among a larger number of employees.

A small staff is a close-knit group. The formalities that may exist in a larger library would be absurd in a small one. The staff will work as a team; there will be a general knowledge on the part of everyone of the personal concerns of everyone else. Informality will to some degree extend to relationships with readers. All this friendly give and take is natural and inevitable. If the degree of informality is properly controlled, the atmosphere

42

of friendliness which it generates adds to the staff's enjoyment of its work and to the public's pleasure when visiting the library.

Nevertheless, the staff is there to work. If informality gets out of hand, if schedule changes and special privileges are heedlessly granted, if friendship reaches the stage where the authority of the librarian is weakened, then the library itself is also weakened. A businesslike, as well as a friendly, attitude is necessary, and it is the librarian's responsibility to establish by his direction and his example the appropriate balance between efficiency and cordiality.

One method of achieving such a balance is a careful assignment of duties and responsibilities. On a small staff there must be flexibility and interchangeability, yet the major responsibility for each job must be given to some one staff member. Just as, on a ball team, each member has his own position to cover, his own job to do, so on the small library team each person should be definitely assigned to be in charge of something or of several things. A clear-cut directive of what is expected of each member, plus a firm—though not totally inflexible—insistence on the observance of rules about schedules, time off, and businesslike behavior in general, will set the right tone and should strengthen, not weaken, team spirit in a good staff. Friendliness and informality can then exist without danger, and the library staff will gain in community respect as well as in self-respect.

Personnel administration includes varied responsibilities. It embraces decisions as to number of staff, selection of staff, working conditions, fringe benefits, assignment of duties, training, and maintenance of morale. These are formidable problems for the average librarian who is a beginning administrator, or to the board unfamiliar with library practice. Training in library school as a rule touches on personnel topics, but with the many aspects of librarianship to be covered usually does not give the new librarian sufficient help in these matters. Experience in a good library is an excellent supplement; in addition, the librarian should turn to his own shelves for books on personnel administration to help him over some of the hurdles that are bound to appear.[1]

[1] Among the many good books available are: Frances Torbert, *Personnel Management in Small Companies* (Los Angeles: Univ. of Calif. Pr., 1959). 102p.; D. R. Davies and R. T. Livingston, *You and Management* (New York: Harper, 1958). 272p.

How Large Should the Staff Be?

Since the library staff is of major importance, its selection is an important problem for the administrator and board. How large a staff does the small library need, and what should its qualifications be?

Existing standards on the subject of staff size are tentative. *Public Library Service*, while emphasizing that many variables enter into an estimate of adequate staff, makes the following recommendations:

One staff member (full-time or equivalent) should be the minimum provision for each 2,500 people in the service area [Standard 127].[2] In calculating staff provisions under this standard, pages should be included but not maintenance personnel.

Existing studies of the nature of library tasks indicate that the professional staff in a library system should be approximately one-third of the total personnel, and the nonprofessional staff (as defined above, excluding maintenance personnel) approximately two-thirds [Standard 107].[3]

In each library system there should be at least one professional staff member for each of the following aspects of library service:

administration
organization and control of materials
information and advisory service for adults
information and advisory service for young adults
information and advisory service for children
extension services [Standard 131].[4]

As the text indicates, these standards refer to library systems. To some degree, therefore, their relevance for the small library depends on the library's membership in a system or on the possibility of its entering one. When the small library is able to become part of a cooperative system, for example, meeting the standard that calls for specialists in various fields ceases to be an unattainable goal and becomes a reasonable expectation.

[2] American Library Association, Public Libraries Division, Co-ordinating Committee on Revision of Public Library Standards, *Public Library Service: A Guide to Evaluation, with Minimum Standards* (Chicago: A.L.A., 1956), p.43.
[3] *Ibid.*, p.39.
[4] *Ibid.*, p.44.

Furthermore, if certain procedures are performed centrally for the system—such as sending overdue notices, processing inter-library loans, or reproducing catalog cards—the ratio of professional to nonprofessional staff may change within the library itself. For the system as a whole, the standard may well be met or exceeded, but the local library that is a system member may find itself able to put more of its salary money into providing professional reference and advisory staff that serves the public directly.

Until the publication of *Interim Standards,* the meeting of standards was not easy for those concerned with the personnel needs of small libraries both in and out of systems. Now the small library has more usable guidelines with which to work. The interim standards, while pointing again to the existence of many variables, spell out suggested minimum staffing patterns for small libraries of various sizes up to those serving populations of just under 50,000.[5] Numbers, general classifications, and educational qualifications are given. The librarian must remember that local variables must be taken into account and that the interim standards do not claim to offer more than interim goals for libraries unable to meet the standards of minimum adequate library service given in *Public Library Service.* The latter is still the only valid statement of standards of minimum adequacy.

On the whole, the interim standards agree with the general standards as to size of staff needed (one staff member or more, exclusive of maintenance staff, for every 2,500 of population served), and as to ratio of professional and nonprofessional staff, with some modifications. They do not attempt to meet the standards of specialization required by *Public Library Service;* in thus accepting the probability that the independent small library usually cannot provide such specialization, they underline one of the chief weaknesses of the average smaller local library.

Existing libraries, especially small ones, are frequently working with staffs that have little relationship to those proposed by either set of standards. Many have only one or two professionals, when by any standard they should have more. It would, therefore, be unrealistic for a book on the administration of the small

[5] American Library Association, Public Library Association, Subcommittee on Standards for Small Libraries, *Interim Standards for Small Public Libraries: Guidelines toward Achieving the Goals of* Public Library Service (Chicago: A.L.A., 1962), p.9–10.

public library to assume the existence of the standard staffing pattern in considering such matters as assignment of duties. It would be indefensible, on the other hand, to accept the existing situation without pointing out that a substandard staff (in numbers or in quality) cannot be expected to give adequate library service, and that it is one of the first obligations of librarian and trustees to bring the staff up to par.

The staff picture varies considerably in smaller libraries with one or two professional librarians. In some libraries, unfortunately, the one or two are the entire staff. In others, especially where the size of the community calls for more personnel, they are joined by a large number of nonprofessionals. According to the tentative minimum standards recommended, the library with one professional should have two nonprofessionals, the one with two professionals should have four nonprofessionals out of a total of six. If there are more professionals than the ratio indicates, one of two possibilities is true: it may be that the library is giving a higher quality of service than the standards call for, or (and in the small library this is more probable) the professionally trained staff is performing far too many tasks that do not require professional training. If, on the other hand, there are more nonprofessionals than the ratio suggests, almost certainly a larger professional force is needed.

Selecting the Professional Staff

For the average small library there comes the time, usually not soon enough, when a second professional librarian is budgeted for. System membership will not postpone the need for a second professional, although it may affect the type of person required. In seeking this important addition to the staff, librarian and board are faced with two immediate problems: what qualifications should be sought and how the best person can be obtained.

There may be a question in the minds of some about the necessity for library school training. In spite of the undoubted fact that one can always point to highly successful untrained people and to less-successful librarians with full credentials, the weight of logic is on the side of professional training. The most common danger for the small library is that it may become ingrown—a possibility which becomes a virtual certainty when the succession is handed down from one librarian to another, with each training the successor and neither having experience or training elsewhere.

A second professional with independently acquired knowledge and a questioning point of view will call for some adjustments and considerable maturity on the part of the librarian who has formerly dealt only with untrained staff members. But in the long run the addition of a newcomer with equal theoretical knowledge, with whom problems can be discussed and who can contribute fresh ideas and approaches, enriches the library's vitality and service and increases the librarian's own status and confidence.

Most small public libraries look for a children's librarian, first, when adding a second professional staff member—a natural choice, especially if the librarian has no special training in or aptitude for children's service. In recruiting and describing the position the librarian must remember that no one can be a total specialist in a small library. It is unfair to the recruit, to the librarian, and to the nonjuvenile public to give the impression in recruiting that such a person can spend full time in work with children or in the community on behalf of children, leaving responsibility for administration, cataloging, supervision, and adult service to the other professional.

In some libraries, especially if the librarian chooses to retain the responsibility for children's work, the second professional may be called a reference librarian or cataloger. Here, again, the title does not describe the whole position. It is well sometimes to call the second professional the assistant librarian rather than to give him a more limiting title, though in this case, too, it is important that he have a specialty and special assignment. Often he may have two. Reference librarian-cataloger is a frequent combination, and even children's librarian-cataloger, although the latter occurs less frequently. Whatever the special assignment, the person must be flexible and adaptable, able to help where help is needed, and not expecting to be able to devote full time to any one service, however important.

To the librarian who has for years assumed all responsibilities, the delegation of one large assignment may seem to promise untold relief and freedom, and he may seek and find a specialist who will do a fine job in one area but sadly unbalance the total service. What the small library needs is a specialist who can also perform with grace additional services as needed. As the professional staff grows, more specialization becomes possible, but no small library can realistically promise total specialization to any new staff member.

Recruiting the Professional Staff

Library schools will usually post notices of openings and are sometimes able to recommend graduates. In the realities of today's competition for staff, however, one's notice shares bulletin-board space with literally hundreds of others and the recommended graduates are in great demand. State library agencies sometimes offer a referral or placement service, and national and state library periodicals accept advertisements. These are the most common means of recruiting a new professional employee. In addition, the annual convention of the American Library Association offers the opportunity of identifying and interviewing applicants. At such meetings, however, one does not find many junior librarians in search of a position.

Small libraries are not usually able to pay the expenses of an applicant for an interview at the library, if there is a long distance involved. Yet an interview is highly desirable. It is sometimes possible to ask another librarian to interview a candidate and send a confidential opinion. References and previous employers should also be queried. In civil service libraries, standard procedure will be followed; in many cases this means an examination: written, oral, or both. During periods of many vacancies and general shortage of librarians, regulations may make the search more difficult. Recruiting for a librarian is normally a nationwide rather than a state or local affair, which further complicates the picture.

The Nonprofessional Staff

The importance of the nonprofessional staff in the small library can scarcely be overestimated. Nonprofessionals, if recommendations are followed, will outnumber the professional librarians. They will be given important assignments and become in every respect full-fledged members of the library team. Selecting and training nonprofessional staff members are, therefore, fully as important as selecting and training librarians.

The nonprofessional staff is normally recruited locally. The standing of the library in the community contributes much to its ability to attract good local personnel. Job opportunities are many and varied in the average community, and the library is in keen competition with other potential employers. Librarian and trustees must try to make library openings as challenging and attractive as possible, so that young people just out of school, and potentially valuable older people with appropriate backgrounds, will want to work in the library, even with the prospect of evening and Saturday hours.

Good staff members are usually ambitious; they know they are capable of assuming responsibility and naturally want positions in which they can advance. The problem of providing career opportunities for the nonprofessional staff in the small library is admittedly a difficult one. If, as *Interim Standards* recommends,[6] the staff includes one or more college graduates with some library courses or experience, and one or more library assistants with at least two years of college and also some library courses or experience, the future of these staff members will be a matter of concern to the librarian. The college graduate may well be considered the equivalent of a preprofessional or trainee in a larger system—that is, a person working in the library pending the completion of professional training. If at all possible, such staff members should be encouraged to continue and complete their library training, so that they may be eligible for promotion in the same library or another. Assistance to them can take such practical forms as help in obtaining scholarships and loans, or arrangement of schedules to permit attendance at a nearby library school. The librarian should be especially alert to the importance of urging full professional training for a staff member who should have the opportunity of being groomed to be his own successor.

The staff member with a good background, some library training, and only a partial college education may also be a good professional prospect, and if so, should be encouraged to make the effort to work toward a professional library career. An alternative road to advancement within the library is business training, with the prospect of becoming supervisor of all business and clerical operations: bookkeeping, statistics, correspondence, circulation work, record-keeping, and the like. A staff member with business training can act as an administrative aide to the librarian, relieving him of many details and thus enabling him to spend more of his time with books and readers.

[6] *Ibid.*

The clerical staff also needs business skills, such as ability to type and keep statistics, plus the qualities necessary to meet the public: tact, good grooming, pleasant manner, correct speech. If there is an administrative aide, the clerical staff will be under her supervision, but she will necessarily delegate to experienced clerks much of the responsibility for handling day-to-day routines, such as overdues, circulation, reserves, and the like.

Developing a Simple Personnel Structure

The small library with its modest staff and informal relationships may seem to have no need for such formidable-sounding apparatus as classification and pay plan, organization chart, and job descriptions. Where there is a city or county personnel officer, however, these are normal and expected patterns for the jurisdiction as a whole. Even when personnel matters are entirely within the discretion of the librarian and trustees, there is value in a regularized structure, although it may be a simple one.

A classification plan exists to give the most specialized work to the most highly skilled and best-trained people, and simpler work to those with less training and experience. It also provides a yardstick for measuring the relative importance of jobs in comparison with others, not only in the library but also elsewhere in community public service. In classifying a position, account is taken not only of the training and experience necessary for adequate performance of a job, but also of the responsibility assumed, the amount of supervision necessary, the number of people supervised, and the relative seriousness of the consequences of error on the job. If, for example, the local superintendent of schools requires more professional training than the librarian and supervises more people, he will probably have a higher classification in the overall community plan, even though the amount of supervision received would be nominal in both cases and the consequences of an error in the budget of either would be equally disastrous. If one clerical worker is in charge of overdues and another of reserves, the two tasks may be considered about equal; on the other hand, the one who spends most of the time on shelving and mending would probably receive a lower classification and lower pay.

Basic to the preparation of a classification plan is the statement of duties required of each job. The statement should list the duties the staff member actually performs after tasks appropriate to the position have been assigned. For example, that of an assistant librarian who is also children's librarian might read as follows:

Supervises library in absence of librarian
Assists with preparation of budget
Supervises service to children
Trains library assistants in work with children
Selects children's books
Supervises library assistant who works with children
Supervises community work with children's organizations
Is responsible for library's relations with schools
Assists in giving reader and reference service to adults and
  young adults
Catalogs children's books
Assists in cataloging adult books

The statement for a library assistant who acts as administrative aide and secretary might contain these duties:

Supervises, under general supervision of librarian, desk as-
  sistants and page
Acts as secretary to librarian and assistant librarian
Assists with typing as needed
Keeps financial records
Keeps circulation and other statistics
Assists with displays and other public relations work
Works at circulation desk as needed
Handles reader complaints about overdues, fines, and the like
Answers telephone and gives preliminary assistance to readers
  during busy periods
Has general responsibility for library routines and makes sug-
  gestions for improved methods

Similar duty statements for each staff member keep clear-cut the duties and responsibilities of each. Details will vary from library to library. These variations are unimportant as long as the basic principle is kept in mind: each member of the staff should spend as much time as possible working on tasks that require skills appropriate for his classification and salary. Duty statements may also be shown on an organization chart, which makes clear at a glance the lines of authority. For the small library with two professionals and six nonprofessionals (one of whom is a college graduate with some library training) the chart might look like the one on page 53, with the blocks made large enough for the duties of each individual to be included.

The samples given of duty statements and organization chart are subject to many modifications. The talents, experience, and abilities of each staff member must be utilized to the fullest in a small library, and duties may be redistributed when there is a change of staff. A new desk assistant, for example, may be able to make beautiful displays—a talent the library cannot afford to disregard. When duties are exchanged, it is important that they be consistent with classification or that classification be reviewed when a significant change occurs. The small library has a problem here that differs from that of the large institution. It is a principle of personnel administration that the position, not the person holding it, be classified; therefore, it is not sound to make or request frequent reclassifications on the basis of special individual talents which will not be expected of the next holders of the same positions. Here, as in many other instances, the librarian must try to achieve a balance between the theoretical ideal and the practical reality. Here, too, the larger system offers a solution by providing natural promotional opportunities for the highly qualified staff member.

It is possible, without violating the basic principles of personnel work, to give extra compensation to staff members with additional educational qualifications *provided* the additional training adds to the value of the staff member. Art training, a year in business school, a year or more of college, a year or more of relevant nonlibrary experience—all these qualifications can enhance a staff member's usefulness, even though his job specification may not require them. The normal way to recognize such additional training or experience is by means of a salary differential, usually a step increase for a year of relevant training or experience. The library should follow a regular policy, approved by the board and committed to writing, and especially—if personnel policy is to mean anything at all—avoid making exceptions.

A classification plan is normally correlated with a pay plan, showing maximum and minimum salaries. Five steps with regular increases are usual in most plans, with the step increase either a fixed sum or a percentage. The latter, usually 5 percent, is more often found where there is civil service or centralized personnel administration. If a fixed sum is used—that is, if each of the step increases for a classification is the same—the amount

ORGANIZATION CHART SHOWING LINES OF AUTHORITY

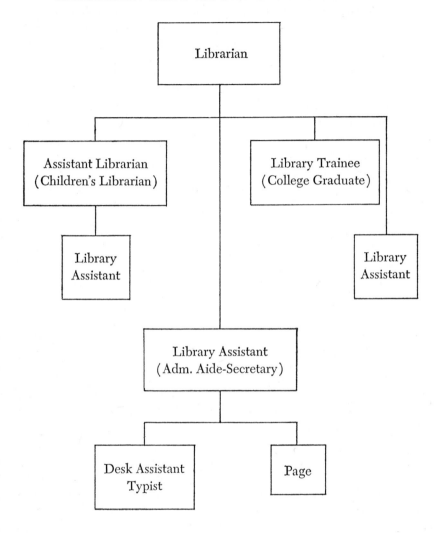

should be large enough to make the maximum salary approximately what it would be if the step increases were calculated at 5 percent. A library with two professional librarians, a college graduate trainee, and five other nonprofessional staff members might have a plan such as the following:

NO. OF POSITIONS	CLASS	WORKING TITLE	SALARY*	STEP INCREASE*
1	Librarian	Librarian	$000–000	$000
1	Assistant Librarian	Children's Librarian	$000–000	$000
1	Library Trainee (col. grad.)	Library Trainee	$000–000	$000
1	Library Assistant IV	Administrative Aide-Secretary	$000–000	$000
2	Library Assistant III	General Assistant	$000–000	$000
1	Library Assistant II	Desk Assistant-Typist	$000–000	$000
1	Library Assistant I	Page	$000–000	$000

* No figures are given, since it would be misleading to attempt to indicate typical salaries and step increases. Such figures go out-of-date very quickly, and there is much variation in different parts of the country, especially in nonprofessional salaries. Current salaries are published in state and national professional journals, and are usually available from state library agencies.

The smaller library would perhaps have only three nonprofessional classes, combining the General Assistant and the Desk Assistant-Typist into one category. Substitute and part-time personnel, particularly important in the small library because of the need to cover vacations and illness and to assist during peak periods, is usually paid on an hourly basis but should also be included in the classification plan and, of course, be provided for in the budget.

Separation of Professional and Nonprofessional Work

One of the first principles of personnel administration calls for the assignment of tasks to staff members according to their respective training, skills, and salaries. If the more highly paid people spend much of their time on work that could be done by someone with less training, they are not justifying the classification of the positions they hold or the salaries they receive. If, on the other hand, people with inadequate training attempt to perform jobs that should be assigned to more highly skilled personnel, the jobs are not as well done as they should be, even though a creditable effort may be made. This principle, applied to the library, means that insofar as is possible, the more highly skilled professional tasks should be performed by the professional staff, and nonprofessional work—including highly skilled nonprofessional work—should be given to nonprofessionals.

Admittedly a complete separation is difficult in the small library. The need to meet schedules and spread among a small staff a variety of jobs that must be done at specific times means that there is inevitable overlapping. The college-trained nonprofessional staff suggested by *Interim Standards*[7] will undoubtedly spend some time assisting with reference service and guidance to readers. In fact, the college graduates will probably be assigned many duties that are professional in nature. There is a danger, however, when partially trained staff spends considerable time with the public, that direct public service will be left too much to this group. The professional staff has much to do; it is tempting to fall into the habit of leaving to capable assistants the floor work with readers, especially when the readers themselves seem completely satisfied. Skilled professional guidance and reference service, however, are among the most important services a library can give. The moment when the reader is helped to find exactly the right book is the focal point toward which all library activities are directed. Careful selection of the book collection, a good catalog, effective publicity—all exist to make possible the right combination of book and reader in the library. The best-qualified staff members must take part whenever they can in this ultimate library service.

[7] *Ibid.*, p.9.

It is not always easy for the librarian of the small library to see the reasons for trying to separate professional and nonprofessional duties or to agree that such a separation is possible. Often the justification for a combination of professional and nonprofessional assignments has no connection with such procedural problems as scheduling. Morale, a desire to promote good will among the staff, a reluctance to create a professional-clerical "caste system"—these are often cited as reasons for giving an equal share of professional duties to nonprofessional staff. Every staff member should take pride in the library and feel that he belongs, but it is a mistake to believe that these attitudes can be fostered among nonprofessionals only by giving them an equal share of professional work. If their work is genuinely recognized as the important part of library service that it is, if they are given responsibility for it, encouraged to develop it and make suggestions for its improvement, and adequately paid for the special skills and knowledge required, there should be no feeling on either side that adherence to a schedule of appropriate division of duties is undemocratic.

Another reason for assignment of duties according to training and skill required is evident in cases where the library fits into a personnel pattern larger than its own, and this happens more and more often as public administration becomes formalized and personnel surveys are made by professional firms. Positions are then classified primarily on the basis of samplings of how each employee expends his time. Regardless of the education needed and the responsibilities carried, a job will be classified as too low for a professional position if the incumbent spends a large proportion of time on tasks requiring little or no training. If there were no other reason to separate professional and nonprofessional work and to assign each to the appropriate staff member, this might be sufficient. But much more important reasons are the efficiency and improvement of service.[8]

Working with a Personnel Officer

In some communities, personnel administration and policy are not solely the responsibility of the librarian and board. A special

[8] See Bernard P. Donnelly and Wesley L. Barker, "Personnel Practices in Setting Salaries for Professional Librarians," *News Notes of California Libraries*, 54:191–94 (Spring, 1959)—a professional personnel official's comments on this subject.

officer, usually a man with professional training in personnel administration, is in charge of overall personnel work for the entire jurisdiction, including the library. Sometimes there is a centralized personnel board or commission. Such centralization almost always occurs where there is civil service, and it is found increasingly in parts of the country where the city manager or county executive system is the usual pattern. Many small jurisdictions have adopted this system or have copied some of its methods, and librarians should be familiar with it.

The personnel officer normally sets up a classification and pay plan for the entire jurisdiction. All library positions will thus be classified by him, and all salaries will be determined in the personnel office. He will review reclassifications requested by the library, prepare job specifications, and set up procedures for employment of new staff members. Under such a system, librarian and board cannot make promotions or raise salaries at will, nor can they independently create new positions. All requests for changes must be carefully justified and will be granted or denied on the basis of their validity as related to the total personnel structure of the city, town, or county. Obviously there is a close coordination between the personnel officer's decisions and the budget. His approval of any budget request involving a significant staff change is normally necessary; when he does approve, the library's chances of obtaining the request from the appropriating authorities are good.

The help of trained and experienced personnel officials can be of great value to the librarian, but he must remember that the existence of such officials does not relieve him of all responsibilities in the field of personnel. Learning how to work with a personnel officer may be difficult for a librarian whose previous experience has included more autonomy in personnel matters, or for a librarian whose government has recently set up its first personnel office. It is easy to make one of two mistakes: either to resist the new system without attempting to understand it, or to abdicate to the personnel office all responsibilities in the field.

A personnel officer is a specialist in personnel. He will turn to the librarian, as a specialist in librarianship, for the information he needs about the library. When he is classifying a position, preparing job specifications, or working on a salary schedule, the information supplied by the librarian will result in the right or wrong classification, good or poor job specification, adequate or inadequate salary schedule. In short, the librarian

58

who works with a personnel officer must know not only librarianship, but also something about personnel administration. To understand the principles on which the personnel officer works, to speak his language, to make clear to him the library's program and needs, are all necessary accomplishments of the effective librarian.

Such a librarian will find a capable personnel officer an ally in many situations. Personnel officers understand the need for special training if the librarian can demonstrate that a job requires it; they are aware of the importance of salary step increases, fringe benefits, in-service training programs. If the library has been the stepchild among the public departments, the help of a professional personnel officer can be especially valuable. When he points out what the librarian and trustees may have been saying for years—that the library staff is underpaid, or that extra compensation should be given for night work—his word, as that of an objective expert, carries weight. Thus, while there may be some disappointments, delays, or frustrations in dealing with a centralized personnel administration, there are also rewards for the librarian who takes the trouble to understand and cooperate with a personnel officer.

Probation and Promotion

Even in the small library, a businesslike procedure calls for some assurance that persons who cannot do satisfactory work will be eliminated from the staff. Problems can arise in the small community when Miss X, known and liked by all, turns out to be inefficient and must be discharged. The library can protect itself in some measure from accusations of unfair and arbitrary action in such cases of dismissal by requiring a probationary period of all new employees. Six months is the usual period, during which time periodic reports of performance are given. Fairness requires that a new person be told where he is not measuring up before probation ends, and such reports are usually given at two-month intervals. Reports should be in writing so that they can be referred to in case there is any doubt that a warning has been given. They should include a statement of the duties of the job and the qualifications needed, the way in which the individual performs the duties and measures up to the qualifications, and a general comment recognizing good work and pointing out where improvement is needed.

Reports after probation are not needed so frequently, but it is wise to make them annually for each staff member. They serve much the same purpose as an annual physical checkup, providing an opportunity to look over the year's work as a whole, to spot and correct weaknesses, and to prescribe remedies. Here, again, is the time to commend staff for work well done, although such praise should not wait for the annual performance report when outstanding work has been turned in during the year. Reports are prepared by the immediate supervisor and should always be accompanied by a personal conference, in which the person whose report is being discussed has an opportunity to ask questions and make comments. While there is less need in the small library for a complex structure of reporting, reviewing, and possible protest, it is part of the librarian's responsibility to see all reports and assure fairness and consistency as much as possible.

Promotional opportunities do not often arise in the small library, especially for the limited professional staff. When a staff member is in line for promotion, performance reports are invaluable in deciding whether he is ready for the new position. Promotion should be kept in mind during periods of staff training and development, so that a staff member is ready when the opportunity arises. On the professional staff, where promotion is less likely, the librarian must be reconciled to the possibility that a professional may wish to leave for a better opportunity elsewhere. Losing a good staff member is never easy, but it is scarcely necessary to say that a recommendation should be given with good grace. It is harder to write a letter expressing doubt about a staff member's potential, but this is equally a professional responsibility. Before writing such a letter, the librarian should try to make sure that no personal bias is involved, and keep in mind that young librarians are frequently capable of rising to new responsibilities when they have the chance.

In-Service Training and Staff Development

On-the-job training is necessarily informal in the small library. The librarian and board, however, can foster development in a number of ways. These include:

Regular staff meetings (when library is closed) to review books and to discuss policy, problems, and matters of general library interest

Written instruction sheets for routine procedures

Orientation checklist for new staff

Opportunity for staff to attend appropriate national and state library conventions, institutes, and workshops

Visits to other libraries

Encouragement of suggestions from staff for improvement of service or simplification of work

Delegation of responsibility for parts of work to each individual, with minimum supervision when experience and skill are assured

Encouragement of staff reading, study, and enrollment in formal courses

Open recognition of good work

An indispensable addition to all training is the example set by the librarian. His attitude, work habits, and enthusiasm for library service will inevitably be reflected in his staff.

Salaries

The devices and procedures listed above are likely to result in a staff with good morale, and may even create such a happy climate that staff members will be willing to remain with the library in the face of better salary opportunities elsewhere. Salary, however, is undoubtedly one of the major morale considerations. As it affects the quality of staff, it is also a major service consideration, and those in charge of setting salaries should be realistic in this regard. Older librarians may remember a time when it was felt by some that staff members concerned about their salaries could not possibly love their work or be properly dedicated. Nowadays, while it is still true that no one enters the profession expecting to make a fortune, it is generally recognized that libraries and librarianship benefit when an adequate and realistic compensation is given for the special knowledge and skill required. The new generation loves its work no less because it expects to be properly paid.

Professional salaries should be set high enough to attract a competent professional staff. When a new junior librarian is needed, recruiting may well be on a nationwide basis as librarians are notoriously a migratory breed. Officials in search of a salary yardstick sometimes survey salaries paid by neighboring libraries. Such a survey, while seemingly logical, may not always give a true picture. If a neighboring librarian is untrained, if he is settled in the community after years of service and intends to retire there, if the librarian is a woman married to a locally employed husband, the salary may well be lower than a replacement for the same position would require. The librarian who refuses to ask for adequate salaries for himself and his staff is thus not only creating a problem when the time comes to seek successors; he is also making it harder for neighboring libraries to recruit. Salaries for beginning librarians should be comparable to those paid to other librarians with equal qualifications on the basis of the current competitive situation.

Nonprofessional salaries are usually based on prevailing scales for similar jobs in the community. Turnover is expensive in training time and in loss of service efficiency. The library must be able to compete for and hold good local personnel. High school graduation should be a minimum requirement for desk personnel, with business courses included or added if possible. The nonprofessional staff must present a good appearance, speak and write correctly, meet the public, deal with complaints, and have some acquaintance with books and authors. In addition, they must be able to type, keep statistics, and be accurate, orderly, and systematic. Top-level nonprofessionals may also have supervisory responsibilities. Not every high school graduate can fill these requirements, and the loss to the library in service is proportionate to the degree they are not met. When satisfactory nonprofessional staff members are found, salary money is well spent that enables the library to keep them.

Working Conditions and Fringe Benefits

Hours of work are generally forty or less and are not to be confused with the hours the library is open. Much of a library's everyday work can go on behind closed doors—is, in fact, more efficiently done when the library is closed. It is unrealistic, in view of today's competition for personnel, to expect the staff to work three or four evenings a week and every Saturday. Many librarians find that they cannot obtain staff if more than two evenings of work are expected. In some libraries, the problem of evening and weekend work is eased by a slightly higher rate of pay for those working on these shifts.

Evening work should be shared and not given exclusively to junior staff. The librarian in charge of service to adults should certainly expect to be on duty one or two evenings a week to assist adults who work during the day. The children's librarian should also be available one or two evenings to serve parents and families who visit the library together.

If the staffing pattern of the library presents difficulties—with, for example, too few people on duty during busy times because of scheduling problems—additional part-time assistance may be needed during busy afternoon and evening hours. Perhaps, too, the hours of opening should be reconsidered after a check of patterns of library use.[9] It is unfair to the public as well as to the staff to spread the latter so thin that they are frantic during rush hours and exhausted afterward.

Schedules should be made regularly, somewhat in advance, and should be adhered to as closely as possible. Unless more urgent administrative or community work forbids, the professional staff should be available to the public at all hours the library is open. Schedules should give staff a variety of work during a working day, with opportunities for coffee breaks and some time away from the public.

If possible, the procedures customary in libraries competing for staff should be followed in matters such as sick leave, retirement benefits, and vacations. These are important morale factors, which may be decisive when a staff member or candidate is considering another position. In setting up fringe benefits, the board should remember that school libraries are in the market for the same library school graduates and that school librarians receive approximately the same benefits as teachers in most communities.

If the board or personnel officer appears unaware of inequities or deficiencies in the library staff's working conditions and benefits, it is clearly a part of the librarian's responsibility to raise these questions. A competent personnel official seldom, however, fails to deal equitably with library personnel in connection with fringe benefits. Normally he is the librarian's ally in bringing library vacations, sick leave, retirement, and the like into line with those of other people employed by the jurisdiction.

To sum up, a library's personnel administration should be businesslike, realistic, and based on policies which are carefully

[9] See also section on "Hours of Service," p.82.

formulated, made known to all staff members, and regularly adhered to. It should strive toward satisfied, developing staff members who like their work and do it well. It should recognize merit, give scope for the development and use of talents, and thereby contribute toward making the library efficient, productive, and a vital force in the community.

Bibliography

American Library Association. Board on Personnel Administration. Subcommittee on Analysis of Library Duties. *Descriptive List of Professional and Nonprofessional Duties in Libraries.* Chicago: A.L.A., 1948. 75p.

――― ――― Subcommittee on Personnel Organization and Procedure. *Personnel Organization and Procedure: A Manual Suggested for Use in Public Libraries.* Chicago: A.L.A., 1952. 58p.

――― Public Library Association. *Public Library Policies—General and Specific.* (Public Library Reporter, no.9) Chicago: A.L.A., 1960. 109p. Includes sample personnel policies, covering such topics as probation, promotion, dismissal, working conditions, sick leave, meeting attendance, p.31–79.

Fay, Adra M. *Supervising Library Personnel.* Chicago: A.L.A., 1950. 23p.

Pope, Herman G. "Classification of Positions," in Martin Lowell, ed., *Personnel Administration in Libraries,* p.32–49. Chicago: Univ. of Chicago Pr., 1946.

Smith, Howard M. "Public Library Personnel," in Roberta Bowler, ed., *Local Public Library Administration,* p.148–76. Chicago: International City Managers' Assn., 1964.

Smith, June S. *The Library Staff.* (Small Libraries Project Pamphlet, no.4) Chicago: A.L.A., 1962. 12p.

Wallace, Sarah Leslie. *Patrons Are People: How To Be a Model Librarian.* rev. and enl. ed. Chicago: A.L.A., 1956. 39p. The last sections, p.27–39, are on staff relationships.

Wight, Edward A. "Separation of Professional and Non-Professional Work in Public Libraries," *California Librarian,* 14:29–32, 107–16 (September, October, 1952).

4

SERVICE TO READERS

Service is the reason for the public library. While this fact may be temporarily obscured by the day-to-day problems of budget, schedules, and emergencies, no good librarian ever forgets that everything done in and for the public library should contribute to service. Budgeting must be conceived in terms of service—how to get the most from the funds available. Book selection, cataloging and classification, building plans—all are, in the long run, pointed toward library service. Certainly all planning, all administration, must be consciously service-centered.

Planning for Library Service

Planning the service for a small library is one of the most difficult of professional assignments. At library school, through reading professional literature, and perhaps through working experience the librarian has learned the principles of good librarianship. He knows the basic requirements of a catalog, the important reference books, and the kinds of service that children, young adults, housewives, businessmen, and community groups should receive. Too often he then finds that, even if his community is providing fairly good support on a per capita basis, he cannot meet what he formerly regarded as the minimum requirements of respectable library practice.

Every librarian with sound training and standards who comes to a library with a small budget is faced with the problem of reconciling theory with reality. The skill that he needs now is one not taught in all library schools—the ability to plan, to balance, and to compromise where it will hurt the least, while at the same time never forgetting that a compromise has been made.

The librarian must plan at several levels. At the top, not forgotten though temporarily shelved, is the vision of the ideal service for the community. It is wise to start here, before coming down to earth and dealing with solid realities, for several reasons. The first is that the librarian should never lose his vision and his high standards, never rest content with his compromises. If he makes a virtue of necessary economies that curtail service, he limits his own future usefulness in his present library and elsewhere. He may even fall into the unprofessional habit of embarrassing his more fortunate library neighbors by comparing his low operating costs favorably with theirs.

A second reason for considering the ideal before grappling with the feasible is that the ideal may not be so unattainable as it at first appears. Perhaps there is a way to reach the quality of service the community should have. Unless this possibility is considered and all avenues explored, how can the librarian be sure? Even if the service contemplated in the vision is far off, it is closer than if no vision existed.

In the third place, an ideal pattern is important for present planning. Unless there are long-range goals, current decisions may be shortsighted. Definite, attainable stages in the progress toward long-range goals can be set, and pride can be taken in the realization of these intermediate objectives. The trustees, staff, and community share in the excitement of such accomplishments without the danger of settling back into complacency and self-satisfaction after partial successes.

In the meantime, the librarian has to make do with what he has. With his plan in mind he asks himself which items are most urgent and which must be deferred. He will first set down what he feels are basic needs. If his resources make even these impossible, his definition of "basic" will have to be modified and his immediate objectives cut back even further. Curtailing plans is a painful process, but it is better than attempting more than can reasonably be hoped for. This realistic current planning does not mean that nothing should be attempted unless it can be done perfectly. On the contrary, it means that much will have to be done less than perfectly. But, insofar as is possible, the extent and nature of the compromises should be defined, always with the conscious knowledge that they are compromises. When such limitations are made clear, the staff is not confronted by an impossible task with resulting frustration and heartache. At the same time it accepts the compromises not as the best possible service, but only as the best possible under existing circumstances.

Patterns of Service

The elements of library service are readers, library staff, and books, the term "books" being used as convenient shorthand for the awkward "library materials." The quality and depth of service depend on the amount of staff involvement in the effort to make books useful to the reader. At one end of the spectrum is the barest minimum service: books are provided, shelved, and listed. The reader selects and finds his own choices and makes use of the staff only for the mechanics of circulation. Even in such a service pattern the staff is involved beyond the circulation function, for behind the appearance of the books on the shelves are the selection, ordering, cataloging, and preparation needed to put them there. Some readers in libraries of all types prefer such minimum service. They want to do their own searching and make their own selections, even when additional service is available. For the benefit of these independent readers, the library must make sure that the collection is well organized so that their self-service will be successful.[1]

Beyond the minimum, libraries offer many levels of staff service to readers. How far the small library will go depends on its objectives and on its resources, especially its staff. Types of service to individuals of all ages, calling for varying degrees of staff involvement, include:

> Helping readers find specific books or sections of shelves
> Teaching readers to use the catalog and simple reference sources
> Advising readers on current selections
> Looking up factual information for readers
> Assisting readers with selections on a long-range, planned basis
> Preparing lists of selected books from which readers can make their own choices
> Engaging in more or less complex searches for information or material on a subject

[1] See Chapter VIII for suggestions about making the library easy to use.

Preparing individual reading courses or bibliographies of
some complexity

The preceding examples are all traditional types of library
service, given for many years to those who visit the library. Less
time-honored, but certainly not new, are services extended to
citizens outside the library walls:

Informing readers of the library's resources via newspaper,
radio, television, and other media
Discussing books and library services at meetings
Setting up displays of books at meetings
Leading or assisting at discussion or reading groups (such as
play-reading groups)
Offering programs in which library books, films, or recordings
are used, either directly or indirectly

Some of these services may take place in the library, though
usually not in the reading room, and include such traditional activities as story hours along with such more recent ones as film
programs.

All these activities are truly library service, if service is defined as making the library's resources useful to the community.
All can be given by small libraries, although some may be given
indirectly through referral or cooperation. No library is too small
to direct the reader to a source of information or to a service it
cannot itself offer. In determining what its service pattern is to
be, a library staff must consider all these levels and decide which
it will undertake itself, which it will supply through cooperation
or system membership, and which it will offer through referral,
whether to another library or to another community resource. In
the making of this decision, the nature of the community and the
accessibility of services elsewhere will be major factors to keep
in mind.

Most small libraries will decide to give, to some degree, a
majority of the services mentioned above. The value and quality
of service will depend on the collection and especially on the
staff's knowledge of the library's resources. To give good advisory
service, a staff must read; to give good reference and information
service, a staff must know its books and how to use them. But
a further skill is also needed. The staff must know also how to
ascertain a reader's tastes and interests and how to make its own

book knowledge available in a way that the reader will accept and welcome.

Service to Children

Children flock to the library, attracted by the opportunity to enjoy a new experience and to help satisfy their curiosity about the exciting world in which they live. They sometimes come in classes, with a teacher, to be introduced to the library as a group. Reaching children and persuading them to come to the library is not usually so difficult a problem as that of reaching adults.

What should the small library try to provide for the children who come? First of all, there must be books. Children's interests are wide, and the book collection should attempt to cover a variety of topics and types of reading. Their tastes are as yet unformed, so that the library has an opportunity to introduce good reading and good illustrations as a matter of course. Children vary greatly in what they wish to explore through books, and some will read surprisingly difficult books on subjects of interest to them. The library, therefore, should not level down the children's collection to too low an average or refuse the unusual child the opportunity to search the entire collection for what he wants.

Secondly, the library must have a friendly and helpful staff. A librarian with special training and aptitude for work with children is the ideal and should be provided if possible. But even when there is a children's librarian, the responsibility for work with children must inevitably be shared in the small library. The desk assistant who helps the first-grader get his first library card must be interested and patient. The librarian responsible primarily for reference work or cataloging will at times help children and must, therefore, have some acquaintance with children's books and take a friendly interest in children's needs. Blended with this knowledge and interest must be a firmness that enforces rules when action becomes necessary.

Also important is the place where children's service is given. A separate room is highly desirable. Children need to feel at home in the library, to be able to find their way around their own book collection, to reach books on shelves of suitable height, and to sit in chairs and work at tables of comfortable proportions. The children's room should make provision for the needs of the very small child as well as of the older one. Attractive, colorful surroundings are desirable and can be provided often at no more cost than a more sober or even forbidding decor.

A children's room should not be a playroom. Shouting, running, loud laughter, sliding on the floor, squirting of water from the fountain, throwing of paper planes, and other such normal activities are not suitable here, and these rules must be made plain. On the other hand, children cannot congregate without making some noise and bustle. They are by nature active, and their voices cannot be expected always to be hushed. The inevitable sounds they make can be distracting to others attempting to read or study, and all possible devices of location and acoustical materials should be used to minimize such noise.

Much library work with children is done on an individual basis. To help each child find the book or information he wants, and to suggest books that will open up new horizons, is the main service of the children's librarian. There are also many opportunities to work with children in groups or as individual members of a group.

Storytelling is a traditional library activity now questioned by some. The development of television programs for children is felt to have lessened interest in and need for the library story-hour. Many good children's programs are on the air, but few provide the child with the magic and intimacy that come from listening to a skillful, "live" storyteller. In the small library, there may not be a staff member who has this skill, and even if the skill is there, it is often difficult to find the time to prepare the stories. Some communities are fortunate enough to have a gifted volunteer or even a branch of the National Story League,[2] and these resources may have to be tapped if the library staff needs help.

Summer reading clubs are also popular in many libraries. Children are encouraged to read during vacation months by means of a game, in which every book read allows the child to move a symbol toward a goal or fill in a section of a card or map. Children's librarians are not in complete agreement about the value of this activity; much depends on the way the reading club is handled. If the element of competition gets out of hand, if the desire to win becomes more important than the reading itself,

[2] National Headquarters is at 5835 Martel Ave., Dallas 6, Texas. The league is interested in the history and narration of folk tales.

such clubs do not contribute much toward the library's goal. But if the children actually read and enjoy the books as well as the play aspect of the club, this activity can be a valuable one during the long summer months. The pattern around which the club is built need not be elaborate; children's librarians and library assistants enjoy thinking up ideas, as a rule, and find others in books. They may have to be restrained from spending too much time in elaborate effects.

If local time and ingenuity are lacking, state library agencies may provide materials for the reading club and will surely have suggestions. Library publications frequently describe ideas that have proved successful elsewhere, and children's librarians in the state or area are usually happy to share their success stories. It is also possible, if time is scarce, to purchase ready-made, packaged materials for reading clubs.[3]

Class visits to the library, visits of the librarian or children's librarian to classrooms, and Scout Merit Badge reading provide other special types of library service to children. When good children's films and recordings are available, film and recording programs can also be scheduled. If a local school includes in its social studies program the opportunity for children to gain actual experience in public agencies, the library can cooperate by accepting a few student volunteer helpers.

If the state library agency has a children's consultant, help in program planning and other types of service to children will be available and should be used. Such help from a state source is necessarily limited, however, by the number of libraries served by the state agency. State consultants can advise, help with planning, and assist in getting programs started and collections built, but their services must not be thought of as a substitute for local provision of library service for children. If the small library is a member of a system which employs a children's consultant, many activities can be planned on a system-wide basis. Story hours, in-service training, summer reading club materials, and assistance in book evaluation are some of the services such a shared specialist can provide. The resources of the system may

---

[3] The *Wilson Library Bulletin* frequently discusses reading clubs. See, e.g., "Summer Reading Programs," *Wilson Library Bulletin*, 36:660–67 (April, 1962). Information about packaged reading club materials may be found in the Buying Guide issue (April 1, annually) of the *Library Journal*, under "Publicity Services and Materials."

include films, recordings, and special collections of children's books available to the library on occasion. Whatever outside resources exist should be utilized to the fullest by the small library in connection with children's service as with other services and activities.

Service to Young Adults

The borrower of high school age is given specialized service in the large library or system that the small library usually cannot match. The library can scarcely be unaware of this age group, however, as it represents a growing and demanding segment of the population. Since most teen-agers are still in school, they are often reached by the library through school or class visits. Even without such contacts, they will almost certainly appear in the library, asking for help with assignments.

The teen-ager is conscious of his graduation from childhood. Even if the small library does no more than set aside a few shelves for teen-age use, these shelves should be separated from the children's section. For the same reason, it is better if the library can arrange not to give the major responsibility for serving high school students to the children's librarian, whom they naturally associate with the past. Nor should the existence of a young adult section or shelf be a hindrance to use of the entire collection by young people. It should be an introduction, not a barrier, to adult reading.

Books on the shelves for young adults should be primarily adult books.[4] Teen-age stories are not enough; they are often rather thin and, for a good reader, dull. Adult books for young people should be carefully selected for interest and pace, but not too carefully scrutinized in an effort to screen out the unsuitable. Obviously some adult books should not be recommended to the young, but before the librarian adopts a protective attitude he should consider whom he is protecting and from what. Today's young people are more mature and sophisticated than their parents were at the same age. It is impossible to protect them from the realities of life of which they are already aware.

[4] A selection of the best adult books for young adults appears regularly in *Top of the News*, the quarterly publication of the Children's Services Division and the Young Adult Services Division of the American Library Association.

72

To refuse young people who may be only a year away from marriage or the Army anything stronger than school or sport stories with a moral is the surest way to drive them from the library forever. It is far better to help them to understand the world they are about to enter, to offer them books that will prepare them for the facts that marriage is not all starry-eyed romance but a human relationship requiring understanding and patience to make it work and that getting and keeping a job, going to college, and being a good citizen take effort and may entail occasional failures and hard knocks.

If the library cannot duplicate the best and most appropriate adult books for a special young adult collection, it may identify those on the regular adult shelves by a symbol that makes them easy to find. Reading lists may help young adults make their selection, and staff knowledge of the books themselves is indispensable.[5] Staff members who work with this age group need to guard against the easy assumption that young people are all alike in their tastes. Nothing could be less true. This exciting, demanding, sometimes overwhelming group is made up of determined individualists, who may talk and dress alike but who are also conscious of themselves *as* selves, in all their uniqueness. Working with them is hard work; it is also stimulating and satisfying.

Relationships with Schools and School Libraries

It is no news to any public librarian, or to any school librarian, that more and more students are making more and more use of the library. Students have always used the public library to some extent and have usually been welcomed and given help. What makes the "student problem" occupy so large a proportion of space in professional journals today is the unprecedented increase both in the numbers of students and in the amounts of materials they need. An increase in use and need ought logically

---

[5] *Book Bait: Detailed Notes on Adult Books Popular with Young People,* comp. for the Association of Young People's Librarians and ed. by Elinor Walker (Chicago: A.L.A., 1957), offers a quick guide to books young adults like and suggests ways of introducing them. *Doors to More Mature Reading: Detailed Notes on Adult Books for Use with Young People,* comp. for the Young Adult Services Division by a committee under the chairmanship of Elinor Walker (Chicago: A.L.A., 1964), is a listing of titles for the older teen-ager, who is ready for more mature books than those listed in *Book Bait.*

to be met by an increase in resources to meet the need, if—as is undoubtedly true in this case—the need is an important one. Yet in very few instances have substantial increases been provided in either school or public library resources.

Without the needed increases in books, staff, and space, librarians have been frantically trying to meet the situation with what they have. Seldom has success been possible, although some libraries have managed better than others. Service to adults has suffered in some libraries; in others, service to students has been arbitrarily limited. Much time has been spent in trying to define the respective roles of school and public libraries—a valid-enough effort but somewhat futile when the combined resources of the two cannot hope to meet the demand. Recent library literature has begun to get at the heart of the problem and to give less attention to peripheral worries. James E. Bryan, in his 1962 inaugural address as President of the American Library Association; Lowell Martin; Margaret Scoggin; and other leaders of the profession have studied and commented on the situation. Entire issues of professional journals, or large sections of them, have been devoted to the topic.[6] From these studies and comments the following points have emerged:

> There is need for a vast increase in library materials available for students
> School libraries in some places are nonexistent; in others, woefully below standard. Good school libraries are desperately needed
> Existing resources, wherever they may be, should be opened up to meet student needs
> The whole community, especially parents, should be drawn into the effort to make adequate provision for students

These are the basic needs. Others, long recognized in library literature, are the necessity for continued cooperation among

[6] James E. Bryan, "Students, Libraries, and the Educational Process," *ALA Bulletin,* 56:707–15 (September, 1962); Lowell Martin, "Relation of Public and School Libraries in Serving Youth," *ALA Bulletin,* 53:112–17 (February, 1959); Margaret C. Scoggin, "Public Libraries and School Libraries: Two Sides of One Coin," *Top of the News,* 11:13–16 (March, 1955); Sara Innis Fenwick, "School and Public Library Relationships," *Library Quarterly,* 30:63–74 (January, 1960). See also the special sections in *Wilson Library Bulletin,* November, 1962; *Library Journal,* October 15, 1962; *ALA Bulletin,* February, 1959.

teachers, school librarians, and public librarians and for definitions of relative responsibilities.

For the administrator of the small public library the problem must be approached on several fronts. Pending the provision of sufficient resources, he must cooperate with teachers and school officials in their efforts to help students, but he should not permit concentration on the problems of students to result in a lowering of the level of service to adults. With his professional colleagues in the school library, he must work for a better understanding of needs by school administrators, by the public at large, and by local officials.

Cooperation is made easier by the fact that the library and the schools have much in common. Both are educational agencies; both employ professionally trained people who normally have common interests and backgrounds. Both serve the community and seek to learn about the community they serve; thus, it is obviously to the advantage of both to share their knowledge. As the schools are usually part of a larger system and have access to information through state, county, or district statistics, as well as through facts learned from the students themselves, the public library may be the chief gainer from this sharing. The library's knowledge of the community's organizations and reading habits, however, is often of interest to schools and related groups such as the P.T.A.

The two agencies also share a common interest in making the best use of their facilities for the growth and development of the youth of the community. Teachers and librarians alike want young people to read, to think, and to learn good citizenship. Both want students to develop good library habits, to use the library, and to know how to use it well.

In view of these common interests, it would seem logical that public libraries and school systems, including school libraries, should cooperate to the fullest. Much cooperation exists, but public librarians tend to be so deeply concerned over the student problem that they sometimes fail to see it in context. The problem is made up of a combination of elements: inadequate resources, limited personnel, a growing population in the student age group, and a change in teaching methods that stresses the use of many sources and reaches toward greater excellence. Public librarians should understand that the problem is not theirs alone, but is shared by teachers, school administrators, and school librarians as well.

The public library staff in a small community has an advantage not enjoyed by those who work in larger urban areas. In the latter it is difficult for the professional personnel to become personally acquainted, and constant turnover seems to defeat what efforts are made. In the smaller community, however, the public and school librarians can know one another and the teachers and administrators as well. Such acquaintance should not be limited to the social level, or to the formal occasions on which all meet as part of the official family. Genuine communication and understanding are possible and should be fostered, so that each side becomes aware of the other's goals, techniques, and problems.

Admittedly, such understanding will not automatically and miraculously produce adequate resources and personnel, but it can assist in developing cooperation in such areas as:

Teaching the use of the library, the catalog, the *Readers' Guide*. Who should teach these skills? When? What coordination will help?

Arranging for class visits to the public library and possibly librarians' visits to school classes. Are such visits feasible? What should be accomplished? By whom? What preparation is desirable on the part of the teacher and what on that of the public librarian?

Agreeing on the amount of help students should receive from public and school librarians. How much can students be expected to do without assistance? Where is the librarian defeating the purpose of the assignment by giving too much help? Where is the teacher expecting too much of the student in view of existing material?

Consulting before assignments are given. Is material available? For how many students? Is it suitable in content and reading level? Is it where students can readily find it or does it require searching through reference books which only the librarian can be expected to know?

If cooperation in these areas of common interest can be even partially achieved, much can be done to relieve the frustrations of students, teachers, and librarians. Such cooperation does not, however, take the place of efforts to achieve adequacy in public and school library resources—still another area in which cooperation can be fruitful.

Because school and public libraries usually serve the same students and because resources of both agencies are limited, citizens interested in efficient government often ask whether both libraries are necessary, and whether it might not be possible to combine the resources of the two for greater efficiency and better utilization of public funds. This is a natural question, but one which indicates a lack of full understanding of the purposes of the two agencies. Although they have much in common, with some inevitable overlapping, and although cooperation is important, public and school libraries perform different functions.[7] The function of each is important in itself, and neither can be performed with complete adequacy by the other.

The school librarian is a member of the school system. He is acquainted with the curriculum, the faculty, and educational aims in general. His clientele is limited to students of a particular school; when they leave school, they cease to use the school library. Use of the public library, on the other hand, should be a lifelong habit. The public librarian advises on individual reading and books related to all kinds of personal interests before, during, and beyond student days. He advises parents about children's reading; suggests to aunts and uncles good books for birthdays; recommends to Scout leaders, Sunday-school teachers, nursery-school leaders, and children's hospitals suitable books for their special needs. His range is broader and more concerned with the whole individual; his work with the student *as* student is only a part of his responsibility.

The desirability of having both school and public libraries being granted, clarification of the role of each and expansion of the facilities of each as needed to fulfill its function should follow. School libraries are considered necessary by the community and by school administrators, but their importance as a factor in the drive toward excellence now being stressed by the schools is not always recognized. New techniques, use of a wider variety of resources, more emphasis on the gifted child—all these trends call for better school libraries. The public library has its role to play in assisting with these educational efforts, but it is a sup-

[7] Amy Winslow and Alice Robinson, "The Public Library and the School Library; Similar Ends but Different Methods," *Top of the News,* 12:40–45 (December, 1955). This article was originally published in the Fall, 1955, issue of *Maryland Libraries* and has been reprinted in many state journals. For a detailed study of attempts to combine school and public libraries, see Ruth M. White, *The School-Housed Public Library—A Survey* (Public Library Reporter, no.11 [Chicago: A.L.A., 1963]). 62p.

plementary one. The major responsibility should be that of the school library.

Pending the development of adequate school libraries, the public library must do what it can to help attain them, work toward cooperation and understanding with school personnel, and give what service it can to the student. The special assignment for an individual, the honors paper, the class visit to the library, the librarian's visit to the class, should be recognized as normal public library responsibilities. The mass assignment, however, cannot be allowed to disrupt public library service to the whole community. Staff time and book budgets must be shared by citizens of all ages, not diverted to the service of one group, however pressing its demands.

Service to Adults

Many small libraries, even those with well-developed service to children, have no planned service for adults. Adults use these libraries; their requests are granted, if possible, and their wishes are considered in book selection. But the service is a day-to-day, haphazard affair.

The librarians themselves are probably unaware of any deficiency in service. But if it were pointed out to them, the following justification might be given:

Adults are old enough to help themselves. They do not need the assistance and guidance given to children

Adults have formed their tastes and know what they want

Because librarians are themselves adults, they are automatically able to serve adults without any special thought or planning

Adults are elusive. They cannot be reached en masse as children can

It is because of a philosophy of adult service such as this that a children's librarian, who finds her own work exciting and creative, thinks of service to adults primarily in terms of finding anything at all on the Civil War for a Civil War buff or selecting something spicy for a bored matron.[8] There are, unfortunately, libraries in which this type of adult service is the only type given.

---

[8] Dorothy Broderick, "Children's Librarians Are People," *Library Journal*, 86:1939–41 (May 15, 1961).

Service to adults does present difficulties. But it does not follow that such service should therefore go by default while the greener fields of children's and teen-age service are cultivated. The good librarian will see in the problems a challenge and a reason for more, not less, study and planning.

Adults shy away from heavyhanded attempts at guidance. The approach of a librarian with book in hand and a gleam in the eye, clearly bent on improving their reading at all costs, will cause them to decamp without delay. But they will usually respond to a friendly interest in their needs, to a request for their opinion about an unusual book, or to a sincere and unpatronizing recommendation of a title the librarian honestly believes they will enjoy. After a few visits they can be encouraged to talk about their tastes and interests and to ask the librarian's advice freely.

Not every adult needs or wants to be taken in hand and assisted. Many prefer to browse and should be permitted to do so without interruption, as long as they know that the librarian's help is available. Nor is it good library service to create so great a dependency on the librarian's judgment that readers lose the capacity to choose for themselves. Librarians are sometimes flattered when a constant reader will take nothing without the librarian's blessing, but it is not to produce such clinging vines that adult service is intended. Reading is, among other things, an exercise of the mind, and library service to adults—in fact, library service to all ages—should strengthen the independent intelligence as well as improve the taste and broaden interests. The librarian can be proud of the reader who cuts the apron strings and ranges out on his own, with newly awakened curiosity and excitement, among the unexplored sections of the shelves. What he finds and takes may well surprise the librarian who has previously suggested his reading, but the librarian can be sure that he will be back to talk about the books he has found for himself.

Helping readers select books of opinion is a particularly sensitive task. Librarians know that they are not supposed to attempt to influence readers' judgment but to encourage thinking and the examination of varying points of view. Here it is easy to tread on dangerous ground, and many librarians virtuously avoid mentioning books that can by any stretch of the imagination be considered controversial. Such timidity is unwarranted. If the reader is interested in a subject, he is entitled to the librarian's professional knowledge of what is in which books and the points of view they espouse. If he understands that the librarian is not proselytizing or promoting, there is no reason why controversial books should not be recommended. Nor should the librarian, the board, or the community at large be shocked into apologetic caution by an occasional complaint. The library that never gets a complaint probably contains very little of today's most vigorous thinking and writing. Some reader would perhaps have complained about Shakespeare, had the library been operating during his lifetime, and surely there would have been letters to the editor about Darwin.

Realism compels the most optimistic librarian to conclude that some adults will never become devoted readers. This does not mean that the library has nothing to offer them, for they will and do use books for practical information and help. In addition to the kinds of information almost everyone needs on occasion—from a dictionary, a grammar book or Amy Vanderbilt, or books on such subjects as child care, removal of stains, care of pets—there are many more specialized needs the library can supply. To find out what they may be, the librarian uses his community knowledge, bringing it up to date by keeping a close eye on the local paper. What is going on among the local organizations? The Methodist Church may be starting a serious adult inquirers' class; has the library materials, and do the Methodists know of them? The P.T.A. is planning a bazaar with a United Nations theme—is the library prepared with books on bazaars and booth construction and with ideas related to UN members? And so on through the club, society, and news columns.

Library work with adults in groups takes many forms and is by no means confined to library-sponsored discussion groups and programs. Providing materials, assisting with program planning, preparing displays or lists of related books for meetings, and book reviewing are the most commonly offered types of service to adult organizations. Whether the library itself will sponsor programs and group activity must be decided in context: what else is going on in the community? how much help can the library find locally? how will the program fit into the total library picture?

Assistance with programs, as well as with other specialized aspects of service to adults, is often available from the state library agency and, even more, through system membership. Such assistance is of great value to the small library that is sorely pressed in its efforts to cope with the complexities and vagaries of the ever elusive adult.

Service to Business and Industry

Most small libraries attempt no special service to business and industry. Although the specialized service extended by larger libraries would be too costly, many small libraries could plan and carry out some useful service directed to this important community group.

In serving business, the librarian begins as with any other group. If he has studied the community, he knows what the pattern of business and industry is—whether the community is a one-industry town, for example, in which many people are employed in one large plant, or whether the chief business activity is composed of small retail and service stores. Whatever the pattern may be, the next step is to find out what kinds of information business needs and uses. Finding out may take a little detective work, especially if the proprietors or managers are not accustomed to turn to the library for help. If asked directly, they are likely to look blank and say that they can think of no service the library could supply.

If the librarian is a customer, he can keep his eyes and ears open while buying. Some subjects of interest are obvious: display of merchandise, supervision of personnel, tax regulations. Most small businesses will use the library's directories of manufacturers and distributors if they know they are there. They will call to ask what company manufactures a product with a given trade name if they realize the library can give this information. If there is a large plant, the personnel manager may inform the librarian of internal training programs for employees and areas in which the library's books might help individuals prepare for promotion.

System membership opens up wider opportunities for service to business. Subscriptions to business magazines and to the indexes that list them are usually beyond the budget of the small library, but they may be possible for a group of small libraries forming a system. Likewise, a richer collection of reference materials and even a librarian with special knowledge of the field may in time be available to the cooperating libraries.

If the library can help business to do a better job, it is helping the community as a whole and helping itself by gaining the support of the business community. Service to business and industry, when experienced for the first time, is often a revelation to the reader who has never before realized the variety and scope of the public library's function. The businessman who makes this discovery often becomes one of the library's most valuable allies.

Staff Attitudes toward Service

In developing and expanding the library's service, the librarian needs the wholehearted cooperation of his staff. Staff attitudes as well as the service pattern may need to be broadened. Staff members who have been accustomed to giving limited service may need a new sense of the excitement and challenge that come from trying to find, somewhere in the collection, the exact book or piece of information a reader needs. Becoming more fully acquainted with the book collection, learning to talk with the reader in order tactfully to learn his needs and reading ability, reaching out into the community to give service, presenting library-sponsored programs, offering to obtain for the reader what is not available locally, even giving service to readers by telephone—all these aspects of library service may seem strange to staff members whose experience has not prepared them to take so active a library role. Staff meetings, staff participation in planning and carrying out the program, genuine enthusiasm on the part of the librarian, and the response of the public to the library's expanded service will help to kindle a matching spark in the staff, without whom the expanded program cannot succeed.

A staff accustomed to considerable busywork may honestly question the expansion of service on the ground that there is no time for it. The librarian owes it to his staff to arrange time for new duties and not to assume too readily that time would be found if the staff were really interested. It is better to enlist the cooperation of the staff in gaining the necessary time through work simplification, use of labor-saving devices and equipment, and examination of routines for possible elimination. During this period of self-study the librarian should stress the library's basic objectives, against which each aspect of the work will be measured for its contribution. For the staff, the result of the joint effort toward efficiency will be a better understanding of goals and priorities, as well as improved work methods. For the librarian, there may well be a deeper appreciation of the actual work accomplished by his staff, a better understanding of the time required even by simplified routines, and a more realistic assessment of the time available for the new program.

Another problem a new administrator may find in a small library is a tendency of staff to give favored treatment to a few readers. In the small library some requests for special privileges can be given consideration. Factors to keep in mind are: is the request reasonable? the borrower trustworthy? the occasion unusual? an unfortunate precedent not likely to be established? But some requests must be refused. For example, such special service as holding out the latest books for a favored reader never has a place in the public library.

Hours of Service

Determining adequate and reasonable hours of service is a problem that the administrator of the small library may find troublesome. Since service is its business, the library must be open when needed. Yet the costs of long hours are high. In dollars and cents, there is expenditure for staff and utilities. In addition, there are the personnel problems attendant on long hours, affecting recruitment, retention, and morale of staff.

The businessman faces a similar though not an identical problem. He cannot afford the expense of keeping his store open for the occasional customer. The library, as a public service agency, cannot look at its schedule in terms of profit and loss, but the librarian can and should ask himself what schedule serves the total public best, given the library's resources of money and staff. If the staff serving the heavy public demand during rush hours is inadequate because some personnel has been shifted to hours when relatively few use the library, total service suffers. Many people may be unserved or poorly served in order that a few may be served at their convenience. Time checks of circulation and library use, and study of community habits and free time, will help the librarian make his decision. The library should be open, and adequately staffed, long enough to be available to everyone in the community at convenient times. If there is insufficient staff, more should be sought. But the small library that is open twelve hours a day, six days a week, is probably open longer than it can afford to be for adequate service.

Publicity as a Service Function

Making known the library's resources is an important part of service. The community that provides a library building, a library staff, and a collection of books has no library service unless building, books, and staff are used. If the library simply exists, to be used by those who seek it out, and makes no effort to tell the taxpayers about the facilities they own and the services to which they are entitled, the community's investment is not being used to the fullest.

Occasionally officials are dubious about any attempt to publicize library service since it is a public resource. They feel it is not ethical for public servants to spend public money in the effort to increase the use of their own services. Basically this reaction arises from uncertainty as to the importance of the public library's function—in actuality and in the community's estimation. No one questions the necessity of stimulating—in fact, requiring—the full use of public schools. Health services, such as vaccination, polio shots, chest X rays and the like, are normally publicized widely, with the full approval of all. Is it not an indication that the library is not felt to be essential, that library service is thought of as a luxury when the obligation of the library to encourage the fullest possible use of its resources is brought into question?

If the library is faced with official disapproval of publicity, its first public relations job is with the officials themselves. In order to succeed here the librarian must make sure of two facts: first, that the library *is* giving a type of service that entitles it to be thought of as essential, and, second, that he himself believes that it is and that the trustees agree. Next comes the problem of clarifying in the minds of officials the library's true function and obligation. Ways of working toward this goal include:

Emphasis, in budget presentation, on the serious use of the library

Invitations to officials to visit the library. Seeing people using the service is much more impressive than any number of statistics

Offering and giving library service to the officials themselves, in connection with their work as well as individually

Emphasis on the educational aspects of library use in the

annual report, so presented that it is attractive and easy to read

Encouragement of any tendency toward formation of a Friends of the Library or equivalent group of citizen users. Officials pay more attention to the testimony of the voters than they do to the librarian's urging on their behalf

Types of publicity appropriate to the small public library include:

Good service. First and foremost in all public relations is the development of a reputation for good service. The satisfied customer is the best advertisement, here as elsewhere. No publicity has much meaning if it is not backed up with performance.

Newspaper stories. The local paper is usually happy to print library news, if it *is* news and presented well. Some local papers assign a reporter to cover the library. Others run library columns and special stories. The regular book column takes time to prepare, and many librarians feel it is not worth the effort. Unless the author writes well and easily, the strain involved in meeting a weekly deadline may result in an increasingly routine and dull column. A column devoted to one or two books may create a demand the library cannot meet. Stories about unusual books, summer reading clubs, programs, new staff members, record-breaking days, and so on are usually welcome. Newspapers often ask for odd or funny stories about library use, but the library should avoid giving the impression that the staff is amused by the public's requests.

Radio and television. Regular radio and television programs are in competition with expensive commercial productions and should not be undertaken by the library unless it is able to spend considerable time and talent in preparation. An occasional guest appearance is good, and spot announcements for radio or TV use are easy to prepare and quite effective.

Displays. The idea of having displays in the library is probably as old as libraries themselves. They are useful to highlight some aspect of the collection or to accent the library's resources on some topic of special current concern. Inside-the-library displays have the disadvantage of reaching only those who are already library users. Whenever possible, outside use of simple displays should be considered. A store, bank, or business firm may offer a window on occasion. An association or club planning a meeting may welcome the suggestion that the library display related books. Displays should be simple, oriented to books, and well done. Amateurish-looking displays, lettering, or posters create an impression of the library that should be avoided. Unless the staff boasts an artist of almost professional caliber, it is better to purchase letters and other prepared display materials.[9]

Reading lists. Preparing and duplicating reading lists are other time-consuming activities that should be done well if done at all. Most small libraries cannot afford to produce many reading lists, but a few brief selections on brightly colored paper are sometimes used with good results. Here, again, staff talents must be considered. Poorly duplicated lists make a bad impression. Lists need not look expensive, but the letters should be clear, the spacing neat, and the books selected carefully.

Annual reports. The official report is usually statistical. It may go first from librarian to trustees, then to the city or county officials. Reports are often sent to the state library agency and of late have been requested by the Library Service Branch of the U.S. Department of Health, Education, and Welfare. Such reports, while necessary, have little interest for the public in their bare statistical form and are of little value as publicity. Many librarians have taken the opportunity afforded by the annual report to give the general public a glimpse of the library's activities. Such reports should not be too long or too detailed. It is better to cover a few points well than to attempt to cover everything. Pictures and pictorial statistics are helpful, and specific examples, if carefully chosen, are better than generalizations. Sometimes the report can be devoted each year to a different aspect of the library. Striking ideas are good, but overcuteness should be avoided.

---

[9] See Kate Coplan, *Poster Ideas and Bulletin Board Techniques for Libraries and Schools* (Dobbs Ferry, N.Y.: Oceana Publications, 1962). 183p. Suppliers of materials for displays are listed in the Buying Guide issue of the *Library Journal* (April 1, annually) under "Publicity Services and Materials."

Programs. If the library gives programs using films, recordings, book reviews, and the like, the programs have a publicity value in addition to their primary purpose. They bring people to the library who may never have come before. With this audience in mind the librarian may take the opportunity to describe library services or display books likely to interest newcomers. The books on display need not necessarily be related to the topic of the meeting to serve this purpose.

Talks. Librarians are much in demand as speakers, and a talk about books or library services serves to point up the library and its activities. Opportunities to speak to groups about special services or to reach organizations with whom the library is eager to make contact should be sought. The librarian, however, should not become known as the last resort of desperate program chairmen, available at the eleventh hour to fill in when a speaker is needed. Women's clubs frequently ask for this service, often for reviews of best sellers. If this problem exists, the librarian may need a regular policy to keep the activity within bounds by limiting the number of talks given during a season, requiring advance notice, and reserving the right to select the topic.

Special weeks. Most libraries make a special effort for Children's Book Week and National Library Week. These observances can be as simple or as complicated as can be managed and afforded, but often a simple celebration is as effective as an elaborate one. Most of the techniques and devices mentioned above can be used on both occasions, and publicity materials are available from the Children's Book Council, Inc., and National Library Week.[10]

Publicity helps. The *Public Relations Reporter,* a monthly bulletin issued by the Public Relations Office of the American Library Association, is rich in ideas for publicity, including suggested radio and TV spot announcements. Several commercial services are also available to help librarians. They contain suggestions about seasonal displays, ideas for exhibits and programs, already prepared spot announcements and press releases, and so on. Busy librar-

[10] Children's Book Council, Inc., 175 Fifth Ave., New York, N.Y. 10010; National Library Week, 58 W. 40th St., New York, N.Y. 10018.

ians without a special flair for this sort of work may find them useful, but the materials should be adapted to fit the local situation.[11]

Cooperation in publicity. Many activities beyond the reach of the individual library can be carried on cooperatively. If only one ambitious display needs to be made each year, or only one radio or television program prepared, the small library may be able to manage it. When each of a group of libraries takes its turn preparing a program that reaches the users of all, all the libraries benefit proportionally. One good display poster or background prepared by each of a dozen libraries may go the rounds, with the result that each has an excellent series of monthly displays all year. A cooperative system of libraries is frequently able to employ a staff member whose duties include special attention to newspaper, radio, and television publicity, and to displays.

Publicity efforts, if worthwhile, increase library use. Every librarian rejoices when the library is used more extensively by more people, but the too eager, publicity-minded librarian can defeat his purpose by spending so much time promoting the library that he has none to devote to the readers he encourages to use it. Here, again, the librarian has need of common sense, perspective, and sound judgment. If publicity is not placed in a separate mental pigeonhole, but is thought of as an important part of the total program of public service and as related to the library's long-range goals, publicity activities assume their rightful place and take on increased meaning and usefulness.

Bibliography

American Library Association. *Library Service to an Aging Population;* an Institute presented by the American Library Association Adult Services Division and the American Library Association Office for Adult Education, ed. by Ruth M. White. (Public Library Reporter, no.10) Chicago: A.L.A., 1960. 60p.

―――― Public Library Association. Committee on Standards for Work with Young Adults in Public Libraries. *Young Adult Services in the Public Library.* Chicago: A.L.A., 1960. 50p.

[11] Listed in the Buying Guide issue of the *Library Journal* (April 1, annually) under "Publicity Services and Materials."

—— —— Subcommittee on Standards for Children's Service. *Standards for Children's Services in Public Libraries.* Chicago: A.L.A., 1964. 24p.

"Children's Services Issue," *Illinois Libraries,* 43:449–554 (September, 1961).

Friedlander, Madeline S. *Leading Film Discussions: A Handbook for Discussion Leaders To Use Films Effectively To Conduct Film Discussion Workshops.* New York: League of Women Voters of the City of New York, 1963. 59p.

Izard, Anne R. "Introducing Individual Books to Individual Readers," *N.Y.L.A. Bulletin,* 9:57–61 (September, 1961). Emphasis is on service to children.

Jacobs, Alma S. "Problems of Small and Medium-sized Public Libraries in Adult Education Programs," *PNLA Bulletin* (Pacific Northwest Library Association), 28:242–44 (July, 1964).

Klimberger, Joseph. "Cooperative Reference Service," *Library Journal,* 85:1525–27 (April 15, 1960).

Lee, Robert. *The Library-Sponsored Discussion Group.* Chicago: A.L.A., 1957. 85p.

Library Service to Adults. Chicago: A.L.A., 1958. 32p. Reprinted from *Minnesota Libraries,* v.19, no.3 (September, 1958).

Lyman, Helen H. *Reader's Guidance Service in a Small Public Library.* (Small Libraries Project Pamphlet, no.8) Chicago: A.L.A., 1962. 8p.

Manley, Marian C. *Library Service to Business: Its Place in the Small City.* Chicago: A.L.A., 1946. 72p.

Nix, Lucile. "Essential Services of the Public Library," in Roberta Bowler, ed., *Local Public Library Administration,* p.241–57. Chicago: International City Managers' Assn., 1964.

Phinney, Eleanor. *Library Adult Education in Action: Five Case Studies.* Chicago: A.L.A., 1956. 182p.

Ragsdale, Winifred. *Children's Services in a Small Public Library.* (Small Libraries Project Pamphlet, no.12) Chicago: A.L.A., 1962. 12p.

Shaw, Spencer C. "Children's Services Operating under 'Systems' Organization," *Library Trends,* 12:38–51 (July, 1963).

Wallace, Sarah Leslie. *Patrons Are People: How To Be a Model Librarian.* rev. and enl. ed. Chicago: A.L.A., 1956. 39p.

Wynn, Barbara L. "Information Unlimited! The Story of the San Joaquin Valley Information Service: A Successful Reference Demonstration," *News Notes of California Libraries,* 58:315–34 (Summer, 1963).

School-Library Relationships

American Library Association. American Association of School Librarians. *Planning School Library Development,* by Mary Frances Kennon and Leila Ann Doyle. Chicago: A.L.A., 1962. 88p.

────── Public Library Association. *Public Library Policies—General and Specific.* (Public Library Reporter, no.9) Chicago: A.L.A., 1960. 109p. Sample policies governing public library relationships with schools, p.80–86.

Publicity and Public Relations

American Library Association. Library Administration Division. Public Relations Section. *Librarians and Trustees—Partners in Public Relations.* Chicago: A.L.A., 1963. 6p.

────── Public Relations Office. *Public Relations Reporter: A Library Public Relations Newsletter.* Includes suggested TV-radio spot announcements and news releases. Issued monthly.

Coplan, Kate. *Effective Library Exhibits: How To Prepare and Promote Good Displays.* Dobbs Ferry, N.Y.: Oceana Publications, 1958. 127p.

Eisner, Joseph. "Write the Program Down," *Wilson Library Bulletin,* 36:538–39 (March, 1962).

Loizeaux, Marie D. *Publicity Primer: An ABC of "Telling All" about the Public Library.* 4th ed. New York: Wilson, 1959. 122p.

Walcott, Marian. *Telling the Library Story.* (Small Libraries Project Pamphlet, no.15) Chicago: A.L.A., 1962. 12p.

Wallace, Sarah Leslie. *Promotion Ideas for Public Libraries.* Chicago: A.L.A., 1953. 82p.

5

THE BOOK COLLECTION

The book collection, supplemented by periodicals and other materials, is the resource with which a library gives its service. Much depends on the care with which the collection is chosen. Librarians, and often trustees as well, will be faced with many questions and not a few pressures: why do we not have more new books? more mysteries? the books I read as a child? One reader will be scandalized by a new novel or play, another will demand the latest racy, rental library sensation. The pigeon fancier, the heraldry enthusiast, the coin collector will all want more than is available on their hobbies, while the believer in world government, the citizen concerned about disarmament or legislative redistricting, the teacher sending her classes for material on science projects—all expect the library to produce material in quantity or depth.

The library which tries to meet these diverse demands without a plan for book selection is often at a loss. No plan will take the place of an adequate budget in providing a good collection, but a careful plan will help the librarian to spend wisely what money there is.

A Book Selection Policy

Much has been written in recent years about the need for a written statement of book selection policy.[1] Emphasis has been

[1] Sample statements and excerpts appear in: American Library Association, Public Library Association, *Public Library Policies—General and Specific* (Public Library Reporter, no.9 [Chicago: A.L.A., 1960]), p.12–18; American Library Association, Public Libraries Division, *Book Selection: Proceedings of a Work Conference* (PLD Reporter, no.4 [Chicago: A.L.A., 1955]), p.50–58.

placed on the value of such a policy in the face of attempts to pressure the library into adding or withdrawing specific books or types of books. For example, policies have been written to spell out the library's stand on controversial material and to assert the library's defense of intellectual freedom. Such limited policies are useful only when pressures arise. While a statement of book selection policy must deal with freedom of selection, in totality it should be a much broader document, covering all the materials purchased and not only the small proportion that may be questioned. As in other aspects of the library, the roots of a book selection policy grow out of the community. Here is a practical use for the information gained from a community study. If the age levels, educational attainments, interests, occupations, and preoccupations of the community are known, facts are available on which to base a meaningful policy.

The basic question, then, in connection with a book selection policy is: what is the community like? The second, closely related, is: what are the library's goals? Given this community, with its diverse interests and needs, the library must decide how many it will try to meet and to what degree. If it cannot provide everything that is desirable, it must determine what it considers most important. These weighty decisions deserve careful thought.

Policy-making is a function of the trustees in most libraries, but, as in all important matters, the librarian is intimately involved. Where a good relationship exists between librarian and board, the library's goals will already have been discussed at some length and the community studied. Full discussion and general agreement will ideally precede any attempt to write out a preliminary book selection policy statement. Such broad principles as the educational purpose of the library, the subordination of the trivial and the nonessential, standards of quality, and the importance of the freedom to read controversial materials should be clarified and accepted.

The actual writing of the policy, in draft form, is usually delegated to the librarian, who shares it with the professional staff. They are the experts who know the practical problems which the policy must meet. In some places, the community itself has a share in the preparation of a policy statement. Specialists are consulted to help frame parts of the statement in their particular fields, and sometimes the draft is presented to responsible groups for their comments and suggestions. These practices have their advantages, especially in the assistance given by experts to library staffs too small to have special knowledge in many subjects. However, a word of caution is necessary. The librarian is the community's paid professional expert on books and libraries; the trustees are the community's representatives who make it possible for the librarian to use his expert knowledge to the community's best advantage. Community help may be sought, community understanding is important, but ultimate responsibility cannot be delegated to the community. Framing a book selection policy is the responsibility of librarian and board together, to be performed with sensitivity to the community's known needs and interests and in the light of the best professional knowledge available.[2]

After the draft has been prepared by the librarian and staff, it will be reviewed and adopted by the trustees with or without revision. Having adopted the policy, the trustees should respect it and uphold it, while the librarian and staff should use it conscientiously as a guide for day-to-day book selection.

Statements vary a great deal in inclusiveness from library to library, but attention is usually given to such considerations as the following:

How much weight should be given to public demand? Some libraries can only be described as "demand-oriented"—an emphasis defended on the ground that the taxpayer who pays the piper has the right to call the tune. Clarification is needed in the definition of "demand." Librarians and trustees who plan a policy are right in giving serious thought to the legitimate place of demand in selection. But is a library meeting its responsibility if it buys enough copies of a mystery by Erle Stanley Gardner or a best-selling popular novel to meet the expressed current demand, when by so doing it fails to purchase a book on electronics, an important reference book, a periodical that will give its readers a deeper insight into world problems, or other materials that will meet an unexpressed but nonetheless real long-range demand?

John Ciardi, writing some years ago in the *Saturday Review*,[3] spoke of the difference between the "vertical audience" and the "horizontal audience" for books. He was pointing out that great

[2] LeRoy Merritt, "Selection of Materials Policy Statements," *News Notes of California Libraries*, 54:269–72 (Summer, 1959).
[3] John Ciardi, "Dialogue with the Audience," *Saturday Review*, 41:10–12 (November 22, 1958).

writing finds its audience through the ages, while the briefly popular work reaches the horizontal audience for the relatively short period of its popularity. In the long run, more people will read the great work, even though its audience at any one time will be smaller than that of the book speaking only to its day.

This distinction, translated into terms of practical library procedure, is helpful. Of course, the library cannot buy only great works that will last for generations; it must have books that are important for today as well. But a best seller's horizontal audience, while impressive during a book's heyday, may last for a very short time indeed. After a year or two, the duplicate copies bought to meet a short-term demand sit on the shelves, while the substantial books of information that were not purchased because there was little demand (and whose purchase price could not be afforded since the best-seller duplicates were bought) would still be in use by a continuing vertical audience. Librarian and trustees must consider, therefore, which kind of demand they will take into account.

Most librarians would agree that some books in demand should not be purchased by the library at all. Poorly written children's books; the shoddy products of the fiction-factory type of publisher who turns out with machinelike regularity unrealistic and badly written romances; unsound, undocumented, or inaccurate books of fact; books that purport to help the reader cure himself of a serious disease or lose weight in ways that to the medical profession seem dangerous—these are types of books that most librarians consider unsuitable for a public library. The policy statement should attempt to indicate standards of quality and authority below which the library will not select, regardless of demand.

Should the library aim for a well-rounded collection? The term "well-rounded collection" sounds impressive. Many a librarian who conscientiously strives to acquire, in reasonably balanced numbers, the books in all fields listed in the standard book selection media, feels that he is doing the best possible job as a book selector. But is there not a contradiction here with the also accepted ideal of a community-centered library? The urban library naturally needs more material on city planning, personnel management in industry, and collective bargaining and relatively less (though always some) on agriculture. The suburban library needs more on gardening, patios, barbecue pits, and do-it-yourself home repair suited to suburban living. If there is only one pigeon fancier in the community that also boasts a whole circle of African-violet enthusiasts, it is manifestly absurd to buy equally on both subjects, however many titles may appear in the standard book lists.

Librarians need not feel guilty when their collections are rich in some fields and sparse in others if they are sure that their community interests are properly represented. They are on firm ground if their choices are based on community study, supplemented by a sensitive awareness of changes in public interest. Thus informed, they are safe in refusing to penalize the many for the sake of one or two. The one or two must not be neglected, however; their needs can be met by system membership, by contracts among libraries with planned collection strengths in each, by interlibrary loan, or by use of statewide resources.

Every library, whatever its size, must make choices. None is large enough or rich enough to buy and to house everything it might legitimately wish to have. These choices are best made consciously, in advance, through a general plan rather than piecemeal as books appear on the market.

How much fiction and nonfiction? Most librarians agree that the distinction sometimes made between fiction and nonfiction is arbitrary. It is not true that all fiction is "recreational" and all nonfiction "educational." In fact, it is not always possible to distinguish between these two uses on the basis of the individual book itself. Good recreational reading, whether fiction or nonfiction, is important and its provision a perfectly normal function of the public library.

Why, then, do some librarians still have a tendency to be pleased with high nonfiction circulation figures and to deplore the amounts of fiction purchased and circulated by some libraries? Is it because some libraries have concentrated too much on fiction, neglecting the information-providing function of the library and forgetting that its educational purpose calls for some good fiction but also for much good nonfiction? The temptation to add a large proportion of fiction is particularly keen for the smaller library faced with many demands for popular reading. The critics probably have these libraries in mind when they seem to decry all fiction.

Their criticism is extreme, and the implication that all non-fiction is automatically good and all fiction of less value, is clearly invalid. Nevertheless, the critics have a point. They are concerned about the image of the public library created in the minds of citizens whose only experience is with collections that are out of balance. Each public library is responsible for the public understanding and support of libraries, since each individual user judges by the library he knows best. As there are many small libraries, serving a total of many people, their responsibility is great. If they stress the recreational function and neglect others, the public image of all libraries is affected. A careful endeavor to supply good nonfiction along with good fiction, to provide information as well as recreation, is one way of meeting this responsibility. As there are many subject areas in nonfiction, the library will ordinarily need to devote a considerably larger proportion of the budget to nonfiction, especially in view of the higher prices of many subject books.

To lay down a hard and fast rule or percentage in the policy statement is not usually possible, but the principle of maintaining the nonfiction collection at a relatively high level should be included. In practice, the percentage of fiction in the average good small library's adult collection ranges from about 30 percent to 40 percent. The larger the total collection, the larger the proportion of nonfiction, as a rule. Many factors influence these proportions, which are presented here as tentative guidelines rather than as generally applicable norms. For example, in a community with a good many adults of lower educational level and background, the habit of pleasure reading is often lacking, and the time for reading is frequently limited. A library serving such readers can encourage the enjoyment of good fiction with a relatively small collection, since people will usually read slowly and take but one book at a time. On the other hand, the library will need a good many books of information, including, for example, elementary self-help books on grammar, spelling, letter writing, and etiquette, as well as how-to books that will aid readers in home repair, low-cost cookery, and the like.

How much depth in subject collections? As the small library cannot ordinarily supply a collection that is well developed in all subject areas, it must contain less on some subjects and more on others. How far can it go in providing materials on those subjects it wishes to emphasize? Are there any subjects in which it is justified in attempting to approach full coverage? One such is local history. Anything written about the local community, and much written about the county and even the state, are normally sought by the local public library. "Sought" is an appropriate word, for it is often necessary to acquire local materials laboriously through unusual sources. Other special interests of the community, whatever they may be, are usually represented in some depth: agriculture, lumbering, or other local industry. A local study group, a dramatic or musical organization, or a hobby club interested in local geography—rock collecting, hunting, mountain climbing—will mean that the library needs a fuller collection in the field concerned.

In addition to these fairly obvious emphases, the librarian will do well to keep in mind the needs of the intellectually curious person. For this type of reader, and he is not always easy to identify, the library needs books in the local collection that stretch the "muscles of the mind." No collection, however small, should be geared solely to the average interest, intelligence, and capacity. It is surprising how many average readers will make the effort to meet the challenge of a more demanding book and come back eagerly for others.

For the same reason, the library should not purchase only the works of tried and true authors—a temptation easy to yield to when the budget is small. The small library admittedly cannot make a wide selection of the work of new poets, novelists, and dramatists, but it should make a conscious effort to add some new works in each category. In selecting the best products of young and vigorous talents, even though those talents are not yet fully developed, the library helps to preserve its own vitality.

To attempt to meet legitimate demand, to have an adequate supply of materials on everyday topics such as child care and home decoration, and to provide unusual and challenging books is not easy for the small library. Many small libraries, therefore, have turned to cooperation in some form to supplement what they themselves can provide.

How many books for different age groups? Some libraries attempt to spell out in detail in their policy statement the proportion of the budget to be set aside for books for children, for young adults, and for adults. A tentative division is needed, but it should usually be the result of annual planning rather than embodied in such a semipermanent document as a book selection policy statement. The statement is one of principle and should be general enough and flexible enough to stand for some time. It should be subject to periodic review and revised if necessary, but a statement that needs too frequent revision can scarcely be dignified with the name of "policy." As the needs of age groups may change with circumstances, such as, for instance, the development of school library service or the influx of new business or industry to the community, it is not usually wise to include in the statement an estimate of exact budget proportions for any one group.

The annual rough division of funds for actual purchasing may follow the suggested proportions in the *Interim Standards for Small Public Libraries*,[4] with local adaptations as needed. Thirty percent of the total book budget for children's books, and from 10–15 percent for books for young adults, are the proposed divisions. The framers of the *Interim Standards* stress the tentative nature of the proportions suggested. The local situation must be taken into account, and in any given year adjustment of the proportions may be necessary to meet unanticipated book needs for one particular age group. In making the tentative annual division of funds, the librarian is unwise to consider only the current use pattern. If, for example, children now use the library heavily and adults do not, the librarian should not necessarily assign a larger segment of the total budget to children's books. To do so is to accept and intensify an unsatisfactory situation. Less money for adult books will mean a less-adequate collection, which in turn will lead to even less adult use. The current pattern of library use should be given some weight in allocation of funds but should not be considered as the major criterion.

Can the same standards be used for selection for different age groups? While some basic principles in the policy will apply alike to selection for children, for young adults, and for adults, there will normally be some variation. Standards of writing and illustration are often considerably higher for the younger age group. Children's tastes are not yet formed, and most children's librarians feel strongly that children will enjoy books of high quality as readily as mediocre ones. Children are exposed to much mediocrity in their daily lives; the library attempts to add the dimension of quality. For this reason poorly written, repetitive, unimaginative series books that carry the same stereotyped characters through one situation after another are frowned upon

[4] American Library Association, Public Library Association, Subcommittee on Standards for Small Libraries, *Interim Standards for Small Public Libraries: Guidelines toward Achieving the Goals of* Public Library Service (Chicago: A.L.A., 1962), p.8.

with impressive unanimity by children's librarians everywhere. A firm statement in the policy is needed here.[5]

If quality standards are high, more copies of fewer titles will be bought for children. This duplication is reasonable, since most good children's books, except those dealing with topics of very current and temporary interest, will appeal to many children over a long time span—that is, to a vertical audience. This long span of interest does not mean, however, that the children's collection should be static, or that it should contain all the books that delighted Mother or even Grandmother. While some great classics go on forever, tastes change with the generations, especially in idiom and illustration. It is today's best books that often speak most vividly to today's children, just as yesterday's books were right for children of a generation ago.

Librarians generally agree that young adults should be recognized *as* adults and introduced as soon as possible to the wide variety of adult reading of interest to this age group. The library that provides for high school users only books written especially for teen-age readers is failing to take advantage of an excellent opportunity to stimulate lifelong reading habits. A few of the better high school stories may be needed to capture the interest of slow or reluctant readers, but to have too many such, or to fail to introduce the good adult story or book of ideas to young people, are sure ways to lose the interest of young adults altogether. The keen, special interest of this group in sports, careers, and the latest hobby must also be kept in mind in book selection.

Stand on controversial books? As was noted on page 91, every policy statement must include the library's stand on controversial books, though it need not be confined to that topic. Here, again, the small library has a more difficult problem than the large one. The Library Bill of Rights states:

1. As a responsibility of library service, books and other reading matter selected should be chosen for values of interest, information and enlightenment of all the people of the community. In no case should any book

---

[5] An amusing account of the writing, publishing, and promotion of children's series books appeared anonymously in *Fortune*, April, 1934, p.86–89, entitled "For It Was Indeed He." It may help librarians explain why they do not buy children's series.

be excluded because of the race or nationality or the political or religious views of the writer.

2. There should be the fullest practicable provision of material presenting all points of view concerning the problems and issues of our times, international, national, and local; and books or other reading matter of sound factual authority should not be proscribed or removed from library shelves because of partisan or doctrinal disapproval.[6]

The small library cannot be expected to represent every shade of opinion on every issue that may be considered controversial. It does, however, have a clear obligation to try to have the best statements it can find on the positions fairly commonly held on issues of importance. It must be impartial in providing campaign biographies of presidential candidates, for example, and in offering material on both sides of major issues of national or local consequence. Impartiality cannot always mean numerical equality. Materials are not always available in equal numbers. Sometimes it is necessary to search for well-defined statements of a position. The fact that material on current affairs quickly goes out of date creates another problem. Pamphlets and periodical articles can often provide better coverage than full-length books, which are somewhat out of date even on publication day when they deal with rapidly changing situations.

Another type of controversial book that may cause even more of a problem for the small library is the modern work, usually a novel, which refers explicitly to sex—frequently in words never uttered in polite society. Many readers find such books offensive, and some believe them to be dangerous for others (not usually for themselves) to read. Some librarians share these beliefs, and some cautiously avoid such purchases.

In considering this problem, the librarian must distinguish between the cheap title written with an eye to the buyer who likes a spicy book, and the work of the serious novelist who has something to say which he feels can be said only frankly or even shockingly. Many serious writers of today have seen or experienced much that is shocking during war or its aftermath, or among the uglier aspects of society from which respectability often averts its eyes. They cannot convey their message without

---

[6] American Library Association, *Library Bill of Rights* (rev. statement; Chicago: A.L.A., 1961). 1p.

shocking the reader, because the shock is the heart of the message.

What these writers have to say may be important, and the library should make it available to those readers who want to understand it. The fact that the words used to convey the message cannot be uttered aloud without embarrassment is irrelevant. Reading is essentially a private matter, a dialogue between author and reader that does not take place face to face. For the woman with a social conscience who has led a sheltered life, for example, the reading of a shocking book may offer the only possible opportunity to learn and understand truly the facts about some forms of human degradation that society must deal with because they exist. As a mother, as a responsible citizen, she may feel the need to know the truth in all its ugliness. The public library that does not afford her the opportunity to learn it, by providing honest and serious works that reveal not only clinical and statistical facts but also the human dimension of human problems, is failing in part of its public responsibility.

Any library that buys only books acceptable to everyone in the community will have very few books. Each reader is privileged to select for himself among the books the library has purchased, and no one is obliged to read what he does not like. It is the clear duty of the librarian, moreover, to select not for himself but for the community as a whole, including the mature, sophisticated adult who is not afraid to enlarge his understanding and experience of the world in which he lives.

Procedures of Book Selection

In the large library many resources of staff, time, and information are available for book selection. While the small library's limitations prevent its selection procedures from being as complex as those of larger libraries, it may, through judicious practices and sustained interest in the collection, perform creditably in this area. Among the advantages the small town librarian has in book selection are closeness to the community, a more complete knowledge of the total book collection, and the possibility of overseeing all aspects of the collection.

In order to decide what the best procedures for his own library may be, the librarian should first decide what optimum ideal procedures should be. In selecting fiction he should know, if possible, the following facts about a book:

What is its purpose?

Is its purpose important?

How well does it accomplish its purpose?

Are characters true to life?

Is the book readable?

For what audience is it intended?

What values are reflected in the novel? (This question does not ask whether all the characters lead blameless lives and speak blameless prose. Such characters might not be true to life in certain situations)

How does it compare with other novels of the same author?

Will the readers who use this particular library enjoy the book?

How will it fit in with the collection already in the library?

Does the library need another book of this particular type?

What does this novel have in its favor that would justify spending part of a small budget to acquire it?

Some of these questions could be answered best by the library staff after a reading of the book, but few small libraries can spare staff time for such preliminary book reviewing, and in most cases they would not be permitted by their dealers to return books which were found, after reading, not to be essential. Reviews and other published information are therefore sought. Many small libraries must rely much of the time on their knowledge of reviewers, of the strengths and weaknesses of reviewing media, and of the reputations of authors and publishers.

Some of the questions raised about novels also apply to the consideration of nonfiction. Since nonfiction is a broad term, however, covering a wide range of subjects and forms from poetry to mathematics, a general list of criteria cannot be made. Questions of accuracy and authority arise in some books, questions of current interest and up-to-dateness in others. Readability and quality of writing are of great importance in some types of nonfiction, less in others.

Reviews of nonfiction also vary in value to librarians. The current, popular reviews assess readability, with some attention to accuracy. The authoritative reviews appear in the learned journals some time after publication. While these specialized appraisals are important, they are largely concerned with content and ordinarily pay little attention to readability and reader interest. For example, these reviews will often give the librarian help in determining the soundness of a book but may fail to recognize the significance, for the general reader, of a good popularization even though it adds no new knowledge in its field. Reviews in general publications seldom give the comparative type of evaluation that is of special use to librarians. Few, for example, would mention a special chapter on a hard-to-find topic, or a table or chart that would be a boon to take care of a recurring request for information. Some nonfiction is seldom reviewed at all; for example, a new book on bricklaying might not receive any notice in the general reviewing media.

Librarians' reviews probably come closest to the ideal. The *Booklist,* the *Library Journal,* the *Horn Book* for children's books, and other sources prepared especially by librarians for librarians—including listings in the various state library journals—are of great value. While there is naturally some variation in quality and usefulness of information, they do reflect librarians' needs. Local specialists on occasion may be called on for an opinion, but the librarian must guard against too close a dependence on such expert views. He must be sure the expert understands not only his own specialty, but also the general reader's needs and the state of the literature in the field.

Reviews are most helpful when used in conjunction with an examination of the book itself. As a rule, however, dealers do not send many approval copies to small libraries, and the time needed for examination of many such titles is usually prohibitive. One good opportunity to see new books occurs at conventions which feature combined book exhibits of the major publishers. Some librarians save sizable portions of their budgets to select substantial books at American Library Association or their state meetings. They consider this opportunity one of the major benefits of conference attendance. Visits to large bookdealers are somewhat less satisfactory, because a busy store with most of its books piled high on tables or shelved behind counters is not the best place to examine, compare, and appraise a large number of titles.

Cooperation among libraries frequently makes possible the receipt of approval copies from a dealer, and also—by spreading the work among a number of librarians—makes examination a feasible project. Such cooperation can be effected in several ways. In a formal system, selection can proceed in much the same manner as in a larger library. Another, more informal, arrangement has proved workable for a group of librarians from several small libraries. The various subjects for review are divided among the combined professional staffs in accordance with their special interests and knowledge. Review copies are requested by and sent to individuals at their respective libraries. Over a period of time, each staff member develops a good background in the subject matter assigned to him and is able to give evaluations of new books based on careful examination and comparison with similar books.

The group meets monthly to discuss the new titles and examine the books. The "expert" answers questions: Will we need this book if we have a certain other title? Will readers who liked such-and-such be likely to enjoy this one? Does the new book cover a certain aspect of its subject in any detail, or contain the answer to a specific question? Not every book needs detailed discussion, and not every library waits for the meeting before ordering significant and needed new titles.

An unexpected fringe benefit has resulted from this procedure—a modified form of cooperative collection building. The librarian who is the group's specialist in a subject may acquire the strongest collection in that field. Since the whole group is acquainted with what has been bought, and since there is considerable interlibrary loan activity, the readers of all the libraries benefit from having available stronger collections in several fields than would have been possible had each library selected alone. Interlibrary loans are more effective when the local librarian not only has a record of what is available in neighboring libraries, made at the meeting or sent by the purchasing library, but also from evaluations and discussions knows something about the books being borrowed. No library depends completely on its neighbors for subject coverage, and in some subject fields no library wishes to specialize. But even when there is to be no strong collection in a field among the participating libraries, the purchase of an expensive title by one may help another to decide not to buy but to borrow it, buying instead another unusual book not held by any library in the group.

Through an arrangement with the dealer, the approval copies wanted by any library are kept by the librarian and billed to that library. Those not wanted by any participant are returned. The dealer is willing to give this special service because of the volume of purchasing power represented by the group.

Another group of librarians, situated farther apart, meets once or twice a year to examine substantial new books not needed for immediate demand. Through an arrangement with a nearby dealer, a collection of books likely to be of interest has been previously chosen by one librarian for the group to consider. The meeting sometimes lasts all day, and the librarians compare notes as to the use of specific books and needs in special fields. A variation of this method assembles books in a subject field; each librarian brings to the meeting that part of his shelf list covering the subject to be discussed. He not only is able to judge from his present holdings whether he needs a book available for examination, but also is often alerted to the value of other titles represented in the shelf lists of other libraries. There is a lively discussion of the merits and uses of the books in all the libraries, as well as of those currently being examined. The meeting sometimes begins with a talk by a subject specialist in the field, who is often a member of the staff of a large library.

Informal arrangements similar to those described above exist among library neighbors in many parts of the country. Participants are usually enthusiastic and feel that their collections and service have benefited greatly. Sometimes a group that has begun with cooperative book evaluation has moved on to joint ordering and processing, thus developing many of the characteristics and advantages of a library system.[7]

Weeding

Because small libraries are continually in need of more books, librarians sometimes find it hard to convince taxpayers and officials, occasionally even librarians and trustees, that some books must be removed from the collection. Especially when the books to be withdrawn seem to be in good condition, questions are likely to be asked: Why is this discarding necessary? Is it not a waste of taxpayers' money? If the books were not used enough to be worn-out, was not a mistake made in purchasing them in the first place?

Some reasons for weeding are obvious, such as lack of space in the library or the poor condition or outdated contents of a book. Two other reasons are especially important in a small library: more attractive shelves for the reader and efficiency for the staff. Dreary shelves full of the same tired books that have

[7] For examples of cooperative evaluation see American Library Association, Public Libraries Division, *Cooperative Practices among Public Libraries* (PLD Reporter, no.5 [Chicago: A.L.A., 1956]), p.33–35.

been there for years are a discouragement to the most hopeful reader. The occasional new and fresh title is lost among them. The librarian searching for material, the page shelving, the clerk filing cards in the catalog, are all wasting time because of the books that are not used and the cards that serve no purpose. A research library is justified in keeping, for the record, many books that may be used only once in a decade. But the small library must be weeded and pruned, lest the weeds overrun it altogether. Pride in the number of volumes in the collection, reluctance to discard public property that may have some monetary value, the faint possibility that someone may ask for a book that has seen its day—all these considerations must be firmly suppressed in favor of the overriding importance of having a library that is alive, attractive, and usable.

What to weed, what to keep, what to replace, arc not easy questions. Experience in the use of the collection, knowledge of the community, and use of standard lists can provide some of the answers. The librarian must also keep in mind the varying rates of obsolescence in different fields. New knowledge is being added in some scientific fields at a rapid pace; thus, many science books become out-of-date relatively soon. Some technical books also age rapidly, while others have a longer life. Books on the repair of cars, refrigerators, radios, and television sets are not necessarily useless in a library because newer models have come on the market and newer books that describe their operation. There may still be in use in the community older cars, refrigerators, radios, and TV sets. Subjects that change more slowly include many of the humanities, but even here caution is necessary. No library should feel that it has adequately covered the later Roman period, for example, because it has a copy of Gibbon. Gibbon should be available as a classic, but the librarian should be aware of new research into the period that has modified some of Gibbon's conclusions.

In general, classics will probably be kept. However, if the library has only poorly printed sets in many volumes, these should be replaced if possible with modern and attractive editions. Nor is it necessary to keep every minor and little-read work of every great writer.

Drastic weeding is called for in the area of current affairs that are no longer topical. Books written during World War II on what to do after victory, old election-campaign volumes, books describing the African situation in the 1940's—these clutter the shelves and in most cases provide misinformation for the seeker after facts. The occasional research worker studying public opinion as it was during a given period, to whom such older books would be useful, will probably seek a larger library. If not, his need can be met through interlibrary loan.

Another reason for weeding is that fashions in reading and writing change. Poetry, drama, and novels of another day, now old-fashioned and seldom read, may ordinarily be discarded without risk. This rule does not apply, of course, to the rare literary work that is recognized as a minor classic even though its popularity may be in temporary eclipse. Equally worth keeping are representative copies of the older works of significant modern authors.

The small library cannot afford to hold on to numerous books merely because they may suddenly return to popularity. Such revivals of interest do occasionally occur. Every librarian knows of books that have staged a comeback as the result of a movie, a play, or mention on television. Librarians who retained them are confirmed in their view that weeding is dangerous, and those who weeded have bitterly regretted it and perhaps resolved to weed less in the future. As a result of such resolves, many libraries have shelves cluttered with books that will never reach Broadway or the movie or TV screen. The catalog is choked with their cards, and operations are hampered by their presence. In general, the error of holding many books for a possible revival of demand is more harmful than the mistake of discarding one that stages a comeback. Should there be a renewed demand, inexpensive editions, often in paperback form, usually become available almost at once. The need for weeding, however, does not mean that a complete housecleaning should be done periodically on the basis of circulation and use alone. Libraries that discarded *Anna and the King of Siam* were withdrawing a good book with a prospect of a long and useful life, even had there been no production of *The King and I*.

Some library systems, lacking a crystal ball to alert them to possible revivals of interest and disliking to take the risk of withdrawing potentially useful but now dormant materials, have found a way to eat their cake and have it, too. They have cooperatively rented inexpensive storage space where all the member libraries may store books of potential future usefulness. Storage is simple; records are kept to a minimum. All libraries of the system may use any book, but no book is stored unless its use is expected to be quite infrequent. Ownership still resides in each library. Through this device the books are still available should they return to popularity, yet they are not preempting valuable space on the library's shelves and in its catalogs.

Standards for weeding should be based on the book selection policy. In fact, experience in weeding is frequently helpful in determining what policies are practical and right. Going through the collection with a critical eye, noting what is poor and should probably never have been added, is good preliminary training for the exacting and precise job of writing down the standards for future purchase.

Disposing of weeded books poses problems of a practical nature and occasionally creates an embarrassing public relations situation. The presence of apparently useful library books on a public dump or awaiting destruction by an incinerator has given many a librarian a bad time with indignant officials and taxpayers. The first step toward solution of the problem is investigation of the legal status. Library books are public property and as such may be subject to special regulations. Secondly, the board must understand the need to weed and adopt a policy recognizing the importance of weeding and of the orderly disposition of unwanted books.

Unwanted books may be sold, given away, or thrown away. If selling is a legal possibility, the library may have regular bargain sales at which the public may obtain books at a modest cost, usually a fixed price per volume regardless of the original cost of the book. Such sales are frowned on as undignified or over-commercial in some libraries; much depends on the nature and atmosphere of the library and its relationship with its community. Weeded books may also be sold to a used-book dealer or in bulk to be pulped. Still-usable books may be given to a hospital or a charitable institution, with the understanding that the recipient may dispose of them in any appropriate way. Occasionally a request for books comes to a state library agency from a library abroad; if the local library's discards seem usable and methods of shipping are not too complex or costly, weeded books may be given to such libraries. Most librarians feel strongly, however, that they should not give badly soiled or outdated books to other institutions. All books that are removed from the collection must be clearly marked to show that they have been withdrawn from the library. Regardless of the method of disposal tried first, there may still be some books that must be destroyed.

It is easier to meet public criticism if the librarian can explain that they are the residue left after usable discards have been disposed of for appropriate use.

Replacement

Replacement is an operation that goes hand in hand with weeding. Shabby, dirty, torn books, or books that have been mutilated or defaced, are found during the systematic weeding process. The easy and sometimes automatic reaction is to replace them if they are in print. Two questions should be asked and answered before identical replacements are ordered: Does the library still need material on this subject? Has newer or better material been published that should be substituted? Only if the first answer is "yes" and the second "no," should replacements be considered.

Collection Building

Selecting new books for purchase, weeding, and replacement are all parts of a larger process—the building of the library's collection. If possible, they should be consciously correlated. Most libraries order new books from the regular book selection aids familiar to all library school graduates and practicing librarians. Since money is scarce, librarians tend to select books they know will be in demand and reserve judgment on standard titles that would be useful but are not needed immediately. They realize that often several good general books on a subject may appear during a publishing season and prefer to wait to choose among them. Thus they develop a file of titles for future consideration, many of which may never be bought if the purchase of currently popular titles consumes too great a proportion of the budget.

A procedure that is used in some libraries helps to prevent this possibility. The librarian continues to order regularly, from normal sources, the current and popular books. Standard titles that may be useful are noted and filed according to Dewey categories in a "wait" file. A monthly schedule is kept for working on each part of the classification. If, for example, the 300's are scheduled in January, this section of the shelves is weeded, bibliographies consulted, the wait file checked, and replacements ordered during that month. In February another class is evaluated. In summer the large categories of fiction and children's books may be scheduled. If the library follows such a plan, the budget is divided among current and popular titles and standard works, the collection is kept fresh and up to date, and the staff learns its resources and is able to give better service.[8]

Bibliography

American Library Association. Intellectual Freedom Committee. *How Libraries and Schools Can Resist Censorship.* Chicago: A.L.A., 1962. 2p. Also published in *ALA Bulletin,* 56:228-29 (March, 1962).

———— Library Administration Division. Small Libraries Project. *Weeding the Small Library Collection.* (Supplement A to Small Libraries Project Pamphlet, no.5) Chicago: A.L.A., 1962. 12p.

Asheim, Lester E. "Problems of Censorship in Book Selection," *Bay State Librarian,* 52:5-9 (Winter, 1962).

Broderick, Dorothy M. "Children's Book Selection for a World in Ferment," *Wilson Library Bulletin,* 36:375-76 (January, 1962).

Castagna, Edwin. "Courage and Cowardice: The Influence of Pressure Groups on Library Collections," *Library Journal,* 88:501-6 (February 1, 1963).

———— "Development of Library Collections," in Roberta Bowler, ed., *Local Public Library Administration,* p.177-94. Chicago: International City Managers' Assn., 1964.

Gregory, Ruth. "Principles behind a Book Selection Policy Statement," *I.L.A. Record,* 10:23-26 (October, 1956).

McClure, Robert C. "Obscenity and the Law," *A.L.A. Bulletin,* 56:806-10 (October, 1962).

Monroe, Margaret E. "The Library's Collection in a Time of Crisis," *Wilson Library Bulletin,* 36:372-74 (January, 1962).

———— "Meeting Demands: A Library Imperative," *Library Journal,* 88:516-18 (February 1, 1963).

[8] Dorothy Sinclair, "Planned Weeding, Replacement, and Collection Building," *News Notes of California Libraries,* 54:321-23 (Fall, 1959).

6

SUPPLEMENTING THE COLLECTION

No library ever seems to have enough books, and the small library surely never does. One of the major problems of the administrator, therefore, is supplementing his collection. Some important methods of adding to the resources available have already been mentioned—cooperation and interlibrary loan—and, of course, the annual effort to obtain a larger budget for materials continues without ceasing. Additional sources of books and materials in other forms to supplement the collection are noted below.

Collections from State Agency or System

Many state library extension agencies distribute collections of books on long-term loan to small libraries. Like other state services, these collections are available to the local library as a right, since local taxpayers contribute to the support of the state agency as well as to the local library's budget. The local library should take advantage of this source of carefully selected books, in most cases already prepared for immediate shelving and circulation. Libraries that are system members often receive regular supplementary collections on a rotating basis as a part of the system's service.

Gifts

It is easy to supplement any library by adding gift books, but not always easy to do so wisely. Gifts have added many good books to many libraries; they have also, unfortunately, added many that should never have reached the shelves. The average gift drive leads to a wholesale cleaning out of attics and is a mixed blessing. The librarian, before agreeing to accept gifts, needs to ask himself whether the cost is greater than the gain. Along with some excellent books that the library will welcome, the drive may produce many of the following unacceptable ones:

Old books whose subject matter is out-of-date

Used college texts with many handwritten marginal comments

Books in poor repair that will not last for more than a few circulations

Books that do not meet the library's standards, such as children's series books, comics, and the like

Best sellers of former years, especially book club choices, of which the library already has sufficient copies

Sets of well-known authors' complete works, in very fine print or so arranged that they cannot be distributed by volume in the collection in their proper places

Books printed on poor paper that will not stand normal use, or very old books whose brittle paper will not last

Among the useful books that may turn up as gifts are the following:

Local history items needed as duplicates or first copies

Out-of-print books which the library wants but has not been able to obtain

Good copies of sound, standard works

Good replacement copies of popular books of long-range appeal

Special items of interest from the library of a hobbyist or retired professor, which will enable the library to add depth to its collection

In considering what the gift policy of a library should be, the librarian should remember that gifts are not actually "free." Some of the costs, usually in expensive staff time, are:

Cost of sorting the gifts and selecting those to keep. Gifts must be selected as carefully as new books, and the added factor of condition must be considered

Cost of cataloging and preparing the gift book. Time spent in making a gift book available must be weighed against its probable usefulness and life span as an active part of the collection

Cost in efficiency to the library. Space occupied by gifts awaiting sorting may be more useful for some other activity. Time spent on gifts may be diverted from necessary day-by-day service or routines

The question of acceptance of gifts is important in public relations. People who make gifts usually do so with the genuine wish to help the library, and it is hard for a donor to understand why the library does not add a book which he has prized. It may seem to the average citizen, unfamiliar with library operations, that the librarian is too particular, arbitrary, or even wasteful. Time is well spent in helping the community to understand the reasons behind these puzzling decisions. The board, Friends of the Library, and other interested groups can render a valuable service if they can encourage worthwhile gifts, tactfully prevent useless and time-consuming ones, and prepare prospective donors for the possibility that their gifts may not be useful to the collection.

Many libraries have been successful in adding important and useful items through the encouragement of gifts of new books or of money for new books. Memorial gifts of library books are increasingly common. Bereaved families will often suggest that friends provide a lasting memorial in the form of a book or a check to the library instead of sending flowers to the funeral. If such gift books are selected by the librarian, it is appropriate to add books that are likely to be lasting, that are beautiful in themselves, and that reflect some interest of the person in whose memory the book is given.

Special-interest groups in the community are frequently pleased to receive the suggestion that they give to the library books in their fields. Service clubs, and organizations such as the junior chamber of commerce, will often welcome an opportunity to make a worthwhile contribution to the community. Occasionally the donor will propose that a special gift, if it involves a number of books, be shelved separately, perhaps in a glass case with a sign acknowledging the source of the collection. These requests for special handling are easy to understand, but isolating a collection impairs its usefulness as a working part of the library's total stock. For unusual and expensive gift collections, a special bookplate identifying each item will serve the same purpose and will usually be as acceptable to the giver.

Sometimes a small library is tempted to accept a gift collection that would be of more value elsewhere. A fine private library on marine biology or on Roman coins may be offered, for example. It is clearly the duty of the librarian and board to resist temptation and direct the would-be donor to a larger library which will make fuller use of such a valuable gift, unless, of course, there is a valid reason why the books would be used locally.

Sincere proponents of special causes or beliefs are often inclined to offer the library quantities of materials in support of their special points of view. Religious groups, pressure groups seeking to obtain or prevent legislation, and political parties are included among these would-be donors. Free subscriptions to periodicals are frequently offered by such partisans. The library, in its desire to represent all sides of a question, may accept some of the items offered, but must take care not to unbalance the collection by accepting too much free material espousing any one point of view. Usually such materials should be clearly labeled "Gift."

Altogether, gifts present many thorny problems. Handled on a day-to-day basis, without a firm policy, they can fill basements with backlogs and staff with frustrations. A written gift policy, which may be part of the book selection policy, helps ward off unwelcome gifts, encourages useful ones, and (hopefully) keeps the librarian out of distressing predicaments while doing both. Such a policy, approved by the board, describes the kinds of gift books the library can use, stressing the importance of condition. It indicates whether or not gifts can be called for by a library messenger (usually not, unless the gift is a large one inspected in advance), and reserves to the library the right to add gifts or not, according to need.

When gifts are offered, the policy is briefly and courteously explained—always, of course, after the would-be donor has been thanked for thinking of the library—and the decision is left to the giver. Some libraries find it helpful to ask donors whether they wish books returned if the library cannot use them; the answer is usually in the negative. Since gifts have not been purchased with public funds, there is usually no legal obstacle to their being given away. The librarian can therefore assure donors that books the library cannot use will be offered to an organization such as the Salvation Army, or to a hospital or other institution.[1]

[1] Samples of library gift policies are included in American Library Association, Public Library Association, *Public Library Policies—General and Specific* (Public Library Reporter, no. 9 [Chicago: A.L.A., 1960]), p.25–30.

Rental Collections

Many libraries add to their collections by purchasing extra copies of popular books, which they rent to readers for a small fee. Some go so far as to include in the rental collection books not available free, but it is more common and more in keeping with the concept of free library service to rent duplicate copies only. Even when only duplicates are involved, there are some librarians and trustees who dislike the idea. Their reasons include the following arguments:

Rental collections may destroy the image of the public library as a *free* library

The presence of rental collections, especially in a small library, overemphasizes the currently popular book, the best seller

Readers who can afford to rent have an advantage, in a public institution, over those who cannot

Rental collections may compete with local commercial rental libraries

In addition to these arguments against the rental collection in principle, there may be other obstacles that will make the establishment of a rental shelf unwise or impracticable. The local economic situation or spending habits may inhibit rentals, or the local or state legal adviser may declare rental collections illegal.

Those who favor a rental shelf point to the following advantages:

Rental collections eventually add to the library's free stock. While not all rental books will become useful additions to the free shelves, some eventually can be transferred as needed duplicates of long-lived titles

Binding money may be saved when former rental copies replace worn-out free copies

More copies of new books, both free and pay, are available at the library. Those who do not care to rent actually benefit, because rentals reduce waiting lists

The librarian ceases to hear so frequently the lament, "The library never seems to have anything new." This consideration is especially appreciated by librarians whose book selection policies limit the amount of the regular budget that can be spent for recreational and popular books in duplicate

Where a rental collection is acceptable, the following precautions should be observed:

The librarian will usually find it wise to purchase the original collection from a gift or other special fund, and to repay the original investment to such a fund as soon as the income has made the collection self-supporting

The existence of a rental collection should never be made an excuse to purchase fewer free copies of new books than would be purchased if it did not exist

Businesslike arrangements for accounting for the rental money should be made

The amount charged should be sufficient to keep the collection at a moderate level, but not so high as to enable the library to acquire a large rental collection out of proportion to the regular free collection. An unduly large rental collection gives an impression of commercialism that is not befitting the library

Care should be taken that rental books are not inadvertently borrowed by readers who are unaware that they are rental copies. Reminders often used include stickers on the book, signs over the shelves, notices on book cards, and cautions by loan desk staff[2]

A rental collection should be kept weeded and the books moving slowly removed to free shelves or discarded

The existence of a rental shelf should not at any time cause the library to depart from its established book selection policy in order to add a popular but poor-quality book

Books Rented for Free Circulation

Another method of providing copies of recent and popular books which is increasingly used by smaller libraries involves the rental of such books by the library from a distribution agency for a fixed sum,[3] with the cost absorbed by the library budget.

---

[2] See p.153 for a method of circulating rentals that avoids confusion.

[3] Agencies are listed in the Buying Guide issue of the *Library Journal* (April 1, annually) under "Rental Libraries."

These books are circulated in the regular way to readers free of charge.

Advantages reported by libraries which use this arrangement include:

> Provision of popular titles in quantity during popularity
>
> Opportunity to return excess books and receive new ones as demand indicates
>
> Savings in processing, as the books come with plastic jackets and, in some cases, book cards prepared to library specifications
>
> Opportunity to purchase books after a certain period for the permanent collection, at a discount considerably larger than that of the regular jobber
>
> Saving in time because of reduced necessity for withdrawals of duplicate copies after popularity has waned
>
> Reduction in the number of copies on the shelves of once popular titles in good condition that pose a problem of space or disposal

There are also dangers inherent in this arrangement, and librarians considering it or already using it should by all means keep the following points in mind. First, participation in such a plan must not relieve the librarian of the responsibility for careful book selection. Books received through such a service must be checked to make sure they meet the library's standards and must be returned if they do not. Secondly, too large a proportion of the budget must not be allocated to this collection. In the long run it is no service to the community to provide it with additional copies of current and popular books at the expense of the more solid and basic materials that form the backbone of the collection.

Paperbacks

The advent of the paperback has been a boon to the small library, enabling it to duplicate popular titles inexpensively and to add to its collection titles it might otherwise be unable to afford. Paperback editions of best sellers are often available only a few months after publication, while there is still a need for duplicates. Uncataloged paperback duplicates are not only inexpensive to add; they can also be withdrawn with little effort when lost or worn-out. Many libraries have been able to change their buying habits by taking advantage of paperback editions of titles likely to be of short-term popularity.

More important than the currently popular books, however, are the so-called "quality" paperbacks. The variety and value of the substantial books available in paper covers increase almost daily as new titles are added to the paperback series issued by a number of regular book publishers. The quality paperback costs more than the average popular one, but far less than the same book in hard covers. Classics, semiclassics, standard works in many fields from philosophy to literary criticism, can all be added to the library at a fraction of their original cost. Not every title available in paperback form however, should be purchased in that format. If hard and long wear is anticipated, the hard-cover edition is a better investment.

The availability of paperbacks may affect library buying in still another way. Since readers can purchase light reading at little cost, many libraries feel less responsibility for supplying it. As a result, some libraries purchase fewer ephemeral titles; others purchase such books as mysteries in paperback editions only, except for the few top-level mystery novels which may be wanted for the permanent collection.

Inexpensive paperbacks, as a rule, should receive inexpensive handling. The occasional significant and relatively more costly title may justify full treatment, but the average paperback is an asset rather than a problem to the small library only if it is kept firmly in its place as an attractive and inexpensive supplement to the hard-cover collection. Acquisition of paperbacks can be simplified by ordering from a news-company dealer. Reports and extensive correspondence about such ephemeral materials are not usually worth the cost in time. Treatment in the library can also be simple—again with the exception of the important title that deserves a place in the regular collection. Duplicates need not be cataloged or shelf-listed, and the minimum preparation for circulation should suffice. Some libraries shelve paperbacks with hard-cover books, but many have found that an attractive display rack, similar perhaps to the ones on which bookstores display their paperback wares, adds a note of color to the library and allows for easy self-selection by the reader.

Periodicals

Periodicals, like books, have many uses and should be chosen for a variety of purposes. Demand, in the sense of popularity, may be the chief criterion for selection, even in libraries that select their books for other reasons; but, as in the case of books, there is often a deeper need than surface demand reveals.

Magazines are often considered as browsing material, provided to attract people with little time or taste for protracted reading. Magazine shelves are sometimes placed near the section of the library that is furnished with comfortable chairs, where people who drop in for an hour or two may conveniently find them; or periodicals are circulated along with general and recreational reading.

These uses are perfectly legitimate provided the periodicals meet the general standards of quality set up for the library's collection as a whole. But the library that stops here is missing the opportunity to expand its resources and services in a way that is particularly appropriate for the small library. Magazines are an important, indeed almost an indispensable, part of the library's information collection—a fact sometimes overlooked by those responsible for selecting the small library's periodicals.

The cost of a year's subscription to the average good general periodical is approximately or not much more than that of a book of nonfiction. The information value of the articles it contains is often notable. Magazine articles are up to date, they are brief, and are frequently written for the average reader. If the periodical is a good one, the articles are well written and authoritative. Often they contain information difficult if not impossible to obtain elsewhere: facts about people recently in the news, current affairs, new inventions, and fads. Furthermore, if the magazines selected are chosen because they are indexed in *Readers' Guide*, this wealth of information is readily accessible. The *Guide*, frequently cumulated into large volumes, opens up the way to a wide variety of subject articles, and material in it can usually be found quickly—a factor of importance to the busy small library's staff.

Some small libraries prefer to select titles indexed in the *Abridged Readers' Guide*, because its more limited list of indexed periodicals seems closer to their own holdings. This list, however, omits a number of excellent periodicals that could well be used by the small library serving as a community information center. While the librarian, in buying magazines, should consider whether they are indexed, it is not necessarily wise to tailor selections to those covered by one particular index. It is far better to consider, first, the library's periodical needs in the light

of the total collection and the community served, selecting indexed periodicals in preference to similar ones that are not indexed, and then deciding on the basis of the magazine list which
index or indexes are needed to make maximum use of the periodicals purchased.

Many small libraries, selecting magazines carefully on the
basis of subject coverage, find that they need the unabridged
Readers' Guide plus other major periodical indices. Two problems that may give the librarian some pause when he considers
the purchase of a larger periodical index are the cost and the
inconvenience of an index which covers many magazines that the
library does not have. Cost is not an important factor as the library pays, on a service basis, only for the indexing it actually
needs. And the inconvenience can be overcome, to some extent,
by posting near the *Readers' Guide* a list of the library's holdings.
Furthermore, this latter "drawback" can actually become an advantage when the library has a contract or system relationship
with other libraries whose holdings supplement its own. Through
the broader indexing available, readers are informed of the existence of material they need which can be used in, or borrowed for them from, another library.

Public Library Service states that a minimum of 300–400
periodical titles currently received should be available within
a library system. *Interim Standards* further points out that even
the smallest library (in a community of less than 2,500 population) should itself subscribe to at least 25 titles and that individual libraries in communities of 25,000 to 49,999, even though
they belong to a regional system, should receive from 100 to 150
titles.[4]

Newspapers

If there is a local newspaper, a complete file should be readily available in the community. Normally, the library is the logical place to find it, although the publisher may maintain the
only file or a duplicate. As files grow larger, many libraries have
discovered that the publisher is happy to turn over to the library the responsibility for housing and servicing them. Some
publishers will supply a free microfilm copy to the local library

---

[4] American Library Association, Public Library Association, *op. cit.*, p.36;
*Interim Standards for Small Public Libraries: Guidelines toward Achiev-
ing the Goals of* Public Library Service (Chicago: A.L.A., 1962), p.8.

in order to be able to refer inquirers there. A film copy means that a reading machine is needed, but the cost of a machine is offset by the saving in storage space, the preservation of unique material, and the ease of consultation. A microfilm reader for use with the local newspaper file may, as the result of a tactful and timely suggestion, be donated by one of the community's service clubs or a similar organization.[5]

Many librarians clip their own copies of the local paper to preserve for easy and frequent use the articles of long-term interest. These clippings are usually filed with pamphlets and may be mounted or assembled in scrapbooks if important.

In addition to local papers, many libraries offer one or more of the following: (1) a metropolitan daily for the nearest large city; (2) a county paper or paper from the county seat; (3) the *Christian Science Monitor,* frequently a gift and an excellent general paper not to be avoided because of the sectarian-sounding title; (4) the Sunday edition of the *New York Times,* which in addition to its valuable news coverage and summaries of the happenings of the week provides indexed "Magazine" and "Book Review" sections. The latter is helpful for book selection as well as for reader use. A few small libraries with good budgets and a special need subscribe to the *Wall Street Journal.*

The daily *New York Times* and its invaluable index may be beyond the reach of many small libraries. Where they can be provided to readers through some type of contract or cooperative agreement, they add greatly to the informational resources of the library. If a microfilm reader has been acquired for use with local newspaper files, acquisition of the easily stored microfilm edition of the *New York Times* should be considered.

Because of their bulk and flimsiness, newspapers other than the local ones are not generally kept for any length of time by smaller libraries but are discarded after the period of greatest usefulness is past. How long such papers are kept will depend on the nature of the use and the space available for both storage and consultation in the library.

Pamphlets

The pamphlet file is important to the small library for a number of reasons. Pamphlets are usually inexpensive and often

[5] See p.165–67 for information on selecting equipment.

free. They can be handled economically without the costs of cataloging and withdrawal. Like periodicals, they contain much material that is hard to find elsewhere. They are usually brief and, being published more quickly than a full-length book, often contain later information. Through a carefully selected pamphlet file the librarian can enrich the collection and ease the strain on the book budget. Subject references in the catalog call attention to the pamphlet material.

The problems connected with pamphlets are not serious but must not be overlooked. Probably the greatest is the temptation to add material of questionable value because it is free. While the cost of adding and withdrawing a gift pamphlet is much less than similar costs for a book, other considerations make it equally important to take a long and careful look at the gift horse in pamphlet form. Acceptance of too many propaganda pamphlets on one aspect of a subject can distort the balance of the pamphlet file. Pamphlets that carry a commercial message may also be questionable, though many are extremely useful. The librarian should check carefully before adding these. A file clogged with pamphlets that are one-sided, overly commercial or misleading, too wordy or difficult to consult (e.g., reprints of speeches), or out-of-date will discourage users and eventually cease to be worth the cost of maintenance. On the other hand, a file that is well indexed and supplied with useful, crisp, information-packed materials will be widely used and appreciated. To keep the file in this condition, it must be weeded frequently.

Treatment of pamphlets varies. Vertical files are often used, with the same standard subject headings as in the catalog; for more current or specialized subjects not found in the regular subject heading list, reference can be made to the *Readers' Guide*. The librarian should have an authority for the subject headings and avoid the use of catchwords that reflect only the thinking of the person assigning them. Pamphlet boxes on the shelves at intervals, near the books on the same subject, are also frequently found. General class numbers can be assigned to pamphlets and to the boxes containing them for ease of shelving and consultation.

Pamphlet binders are used in some libraries; they are valuable for the occasional pamphlet containing important information that will probably be needed for a long time, for example, a pamphlet on a local topic. For most pamphlets binders are not necessary. They add to the expense of maintaining the collection, often obscure an attractive cover, and make identification of individual items difficult by dressing all pamphlets in the same anonymous covering.

Besides the pamphlets themselves, the pamphlet file or collection may contain several other categories of material. Documents in pamphlet form are usually treated as pamphlets, as are folded maps. Pictures are included in the pamphlet file in most small libraries that attempt to provide separate pictures at all. Although pictures are asked for and some excellent small libraries maintain helpful separate picture files, the cost of such a file in time and effort must be weighed carefully against its usefulness. Here, as in so many other cases, the librarian must ask: Could the time spent on such a file be more profitably spent on some other aspect of work? If no picture file is maintained, books and periodicals will afford useful sources for pictures.

Parenthetically, in some communities a local art museum or gallery offers framed pictures for home decoration, either free or for a small rental. When this service is not available, the library may possibly maintain a collection of pictures for home use. Reproductions or originals may be lent, a rental fee charged, and the fee applied to the eventual purchase of the picture if the borrower so desires.

Documents

Publications of government agencies are uniquely important because of their official and authoritative nature. They are normally less expensive than comparable books, pamphlets, and periodicals published commercially and are a valuable addition to the small library. The extent of the library's responsibility for furnishing documents will depend to some degree on the distance its readers have to go to the nearest library designated as a depository for United States government publications. The librarian should be aware of this depository collection, wherever it is, and refer readers there to consult documentary materials not available locally.

As in the selection of all types of materials, the needs of the area will determine what kinds of documents are acquired. Census tracts and reports, the analysis of the state population, general statistical materials, yearbooks in such fields as agriculture and mines, government directories and explanations of federal operation, are all useful and should be acquired regularly. In addition, the many valuable and practical government pamphlet series should be checked. Current affairs materials are covered in brief pamphlet series of the U.S. State and U.S. Commerce departments; and the renowned pamphlets of the U.S. Department of Agriculture cover an amazing variety of farm and home topics.

The simplest way to pay for these government publications is to purchase coupons from the Superintendent of Documents in advance. Selections may be made from *Selected United States Government Publications,* issued semimonthly; from the irregularly issued *Price Lists* of documents on specific subjects;[6] and from the listings in library publications such as the American Library Association *Booklist.* Some documents may be available through the area's Congressmen.

State and local documents are valuable, but sometimes difficult to obtain. For state publications the state library agency is the best source of information or distribution. Good relations with local and county officials will help alert them to the library's need for local material.

Few small libraries give special treatment to documents. Those in book form are cataloged with the regular collection, government periodicals are placed with the magazines, and government pamphlets with other pamphlets. If the library has the *Monthly Catalog of United States Government Publications,*[6] however, and wishes to use its index, the United States documents may be filed by issuing body. Not many small libraries hold enough documents to feel that this separation from the regular collection is warranted.

Recordings

Whether or not the small library should establish a recordings collection is a moot question. Those who favor recordings point out the following advantages:

Recordings are a form of communication just as legitimate in a library collection as books. Libraries have books of music and books on learning foreign languages. In both these areas recordings add a dimension that no book can provide

---

[6] Issued by the Supt. of Documents, U.S. Govt. Print. Off., Washington, D.C. 20402.

Recordings draw many people to the library who might not come otherwise. Once there, they borrow books as well as recordings

Recordings are almost sure to please. Libraries which have such collections report almost unanimously that customers are delighted with the opportunity to make use of them. Thus recordings make many friends for the library and have a definite public relations value

On the negative side the following arguments are made:

Selections of a small recordings collection are constantly out and thus result in more frustration than satisfaction. On the other hand, a large or sizable collection may make considerable inroads in the book budget and thus prevent the library from purchasing a number of useful books. In a small library with a limited book budget, this loss of book purchasing power may be serious

Recordings require special shelving and special handling. Ideally, they should be inspected when returned and cleaned before circulating. These operations are time-consuming

Recordings are frequently damaged or worn through use with the wrong or broken needles. Such damage is not always detectable at the time of return

Both proponents and opponents make legitimate points, and no decision is completely satisfactory in terms of either-or. Librarians that have recordings do not deny that they would like to have more books; those who buy only books do not deny that they would like recordings, too.

Several approaches to the provision of recordings in the library are possible. A recordings collection may be started and gradually built up through gifts and rentals. Gifts of money to purchase the original stock are often available from clubs and other organizations or from individuals. Music lovers, in particular, are not unwilling to pay a small fee to borrow recordings for a short-term loan. After a time, the collection grows and becomes self-supporting, with older recordings still in usable condition becoming available for free loan. Some librarians, officials, and boards have objections in principle to the renting of any materials by a free library. Some jurisdictions require all income to be returned to the general fund. If these difficulties do not exist or can be overcome, the gift and rental method of acquiring a rental collection may be considered.

It may be possible to have a sum of money appropriated for the sole purpose of purchasing recordings so that the library need not make inroads in the book budget in order to supply them.

Or perhaps the library can join, or help to create, a system that can afford both a fine collection of recordings and a superior book stock, or can contract, for a fee, with a nearby library for the use of its recordings by local borrowers. Such a contract might reduce the book fund to some extent, but the total cost in money and time would probably be less than that of starting an individual recordings collection. This expedient might create a demand for recordings locally that would lead to public support for funds for a recordings collection in a future budget.

Once a recordings collection is decided upon, a selection policy is needed, and the principles of such a policy follow closely those of a book selection policy. The community's wants and interests are considered, and the needs in this particular area measured against the library's total objectives in order to decide how many recordings are to be obtained and what kinds.

Musical recordings are usually the first, sometimes the only, ones purchased. As with books, the library must consider a variety of tastes and try to select the best. Classical music, religious music, marches, children's recordings, outstanding jazz records, a few good musical comedies, examples of outstanding performers both vocal and instrumental—these are types most frequently purchased. Language recordings are often bought to be used with books or separately. Documentary recordings of actual speeches or events are of interest, as are performances of Shakespearean plays or other important dramas. For many, listening to the reading of a play, or of poetry by the poet himself, is a far richer experience than the reading of the same work. Other kinds of recordings available vary from birdcalls (which no book can adequately reproduce) to shorthand practice dictation.

Not many small libraries, operating completely independently, can acquire an adequate collection of all these types, and these are but samples. But there can be no doubt that recordings enrich a library's collection, provide a much-appreciated service, and afford an additional opportunity to serve not only individuals but also, and especially, groups of readers.

Films

Few, if any, small libraries attempt to build up their own film collections. For them the question is not whether to try to purchase films independently, for this is usually impractical because of the high cost of the individual print. Rather the question is whether to join some kind of film cooperative and, if so, what kind.

The circuit and the cooperative lending service are the two kinds most frequently encountered, and each has several variations. In some areas, there is only one source available, and the small library must ask whether the cost of participating is justified.

Film circuits are usually comprised of a group of libraries which jointly own a number of films, supported by a fixed annual charge or membership fee paid by each member library. If possible, there is a joint preview and selection meeting, held annually or semiannually and attended by representatives of all libraries or by an elected committee. Films are sent on a fixed schedule to libraries, in turn, for a period of one to three months as a rule. The individual library is responsible for sending them on to the next member after the period has expired, and receives its next shipment from another member.

An effort is made in the scheduling to see that each member receives a variety of subjects and that new films are fairly shared. Circuit membership thus enables libraries to have the use of many films which they could not otherwise afford, to offer library film programs, and to give a much-enjoyed service to community groups. If the scheduling is done well in advance, program planning can be geared to what is available for a given date. The drawback to this type of film sharing is that it is usually impossible for a library to have a particular film for a special occasion. Seasonal films obviously cannot be available to all at appropriate times, nor can films that fit in with current events of importance, and program planning is handicapped by the need either to dovetail with the availability of a film or to do without one.

The other type of film cooperative avoids these drawbacks to some extent, but it is most successful in a rather limited area or where quick communication is possible. In this type of cooperative, the libraries again contribute and again select jointly. The films may be owned jointly by the group (as they often are in the case of a system that has other cooperative features), or they may be owned by each individual library but made freely available to the users of all. In the former arrangement, the films are usually housed in one place, where facilities for inspection, repair, and booking are centered. In the latter, each library houses and cares for its own films, lends them freely on request to the others, and borrows from the others in turn. In each case, a catalog with a title and subject approach is essential for selection purposes. If each library houses its own films, the catalog must also show locations.

Some state agencies operate film centers, through which local libraries may borrow from a large collection. This arrangement, usually the least expensive for the small library, works best when the library staff is aware of what is available and publicizes the service in the community. Booking well in advance is necessary, and previewing is not always possible.

Even libraries that have no immediate access to films can make available to the public information about films that can be rented or borrowed free from local or nearby sources. Here, as in the case of books, the library's service must not be confined to what is available within its walls or even within its power to obtain. The small library that stops with "Sorry, we do not have it," and fails to add, "But we can try to get it for you," or "We can suggest ways in which you can get it," is building barriers which confine itself and its readers instead of opening highways to increase the breadth of vision of both.

Bibliography

American Library Association. Library Administration Division. Small Libraries Project. *The Vertical File.* (Supplement C to Small Libraries Project Pamphlet, no.9) Chicago: A.L.A., 1963. 4p.

———— Public Libraries Division. *Public Library Use of Paper-bound Books.* (PLD Reporter, no.1) Chicago: A.L.A., 1954. 50p.

Houle, C. O. "Two Revolutions and Their Consequences," *ALA Bulletin,* 56:652–62 (July, 1962). Use of paperbacks.

Kusler, Alan. "Rental Collections: Pro and Con," *Library Journal,* 84:1753–57 (June 1, 1959).

"Paperbacks and Public Library Policies," *Library Journal,* 86:1831–39 (May 15, 1961). Brings up to date the PLD Reporter study.

Van Beynum, William J. "Swap Group," *Wilson Library Bulletin*, 32:646–48 (May, 1958).

Recordings

Hanna, E. F. "First Steps toward a Record Collection," *Illinois Libraries*, 44:134–50 (February, 1962).

Pearson, Mary D. *Recordings in the Public Library*. Chicago: A.L.A., 1963. 153p.

Quinley, W. J., and Farrell, E. J. "On Record: A Manual on Starting a Record Collection," *Retail Bookseller*, 55:23–26, 29–31, 27–29 (May–July, 1952).

Films

American Library Association. Office for Adult Education. *Cooperative Film Services in Public Libraries* . . . Prepared by Patricia Blair Cory and Violet F. Myer. Chicago: A.L.A., 1956. 127p.

De Young, Charles D. "Report of Illinois Film Cooperatives," *Illinois Libraries*, 45:78–81 (February, 1963).

Frantz, John C. "16mm Film Programming for Small Public Libraries," *Wisconsin Library Bulletin*, 53:327–36 (March–April, 1957).

Goshkin, Ida. "The Why and How of Film Circuits," *ALA Bulletin*, 55:545–48 (June, 1961).

7

TECHNICAL PROCESSES

Under the rather formidable-sounding heading of "technical processes" are normally grouped all the operations that are necessary to acquire the library's collection, prepare it for use, and keep it in usable condition. Circulation routines may be included also. The emphasis placed on these aspects of librarianship varies considerably in small libraries. In some, attention to the traditional concepts of order and exactness leads to tidy and complete circulation statistics, detailed catalogs, and business operations buttressed by records of every transaction for years back, neatly indexed. In others, a desire to avoid time-consuming detail in order to give personal service causes sporadic ordering, confusing catalogs, piles of untouched cataloging, and unfiled cards.

One can sympathize with the motives that prompt both these extremes of attention to processing. If good service is to be given, books must be acquired and prepared for use promptly and efficiently. They must be on the shelves and easy to locate, not in the back room awaiting cataloging, clearing of records, or mending. The community's investment in its book collection cannot fully be realized unless the catalog and classification make easily available not only the specific books in the library, but also the contents of the books. Equally important for service, however, is the need to have staff members, familiar with the collection, available to assist the public. If the staff are not on hand to help readers find the books and information they need, but are too often in the workroom attending to the collection, the community's investment is again only partially realized.

The dilemma of the small library without enough staff to attend adequately to both books and readers has not escaped the attention of the profession. In few areas of librarianship have there been greater changes in recent years than in technical processes. Much of the new thinking has been directed specifically toward the problems of the small library. If, therefore, a library has been content to continue without question the methods of the past, it needs now to make an intelligent study of new possibilities. In considering the path to be taken, the librarian will want to explore two approaches: having the work done outside the library and performing more efficiently the work done within.

Processing Centers and Commercial Services

The small library of today can sidestep the problem of balancing inadequate time between book preparation and public service by utilizing one or more of the processing services available outside the library. These include: (1) commercial distributors which supply books ordered by the library completely or partially ready for use, with call numbers, plastic jackets, and circulation apparatus already in place, if desired, and catalog cards ready for filing, and (2) library-operated processing centers which perform all or part of the work of ordering, cataloging, and preparing books for use. Processing centers may be operated by the state library agency, by a library system, by a larger library, or cooperatively by a group of libraries. Normally they are not concerned with selection of titles, although they may prepare and distribute book evaluations as an aid to selection. Many processing centers place orders for member libraries; practically all centers classify, catalog, and prepare books for use.

Advantages of the use of outside technical services are obvious. Chief among them is the saving of time. More time is available for public service, at no cost in effectiveness of service. The time spent by many small libraries in individual preparation of the same books has long been deplored as wasteful duplication; each library has been doing the same checking, the same classifying, the same cataloging. It seems eminently reasonable that these tasks should be performed centrally. When centralized, the work can be done by experts, with the advantages of machines and equipment that improve efficiency. Special printed tools, such as the Library of Congress printed catalog, can be purchased for a good-sized centralized processing operation. If books are purchased centrally, there may be an increased discount because of the larger volume of orders.

In selecting the outside processing service for the library, the following factors should be considered:

Cost. The sum paid for the service is easy to compute and may at first glance seem high to the librarian and especially to the trustees. Much more difficult to estimate, but a part of the total picture, is the cost of the local work the service replaces. An honest check of the total staff time that goes into processing, and of the salaries that time represents, is likely to prove an eye opener. Cost of supplies and equipment is also a factor, but a minor one. The value of the library service that could be given during the processing time cannot be measured in dollars and cents but must be taken into account—is, in fact, the chief factor to be considered. Another intangible often overlooked is the value to the library, in service and efficiency, of the space occupied by processing work. Comparative costs of the various services available must be weighed, with consideration of the variations in the amount and quality of service as well as the actual price.

Quality of service. A number of factors affect the kind of service the library needs. Relatively minor, though not completely irrelevant, are such considerations as appearance of catalog cards and quality of card stock. The type of cataloging and classification supplied is the major quality consideration. The service that provides the most detailed cataloging and the longest call numbers is not necessarily the best. In considering the library's needs, the librarian must remind himself that the function of the catalog and call number is to make possible the quick location of specific books and to make easily accessible the information inside the books. The services under consideration should be measured against their effectiveness in performing these functions for the particular library concerned. Fullness of descriptive cataloging may contribute little, and length of call number may even be a hindrance, in some libraries.

Coverage. If the service offered is limited as to the titles or types of books it supplies, its usefulness is correspondingly limited. If the books available through the service include all or most of those the library would purchase, this limitation causes no problem. If, however, many important titles are not supplied, the service could provide only a supplement to local processing. The commercial service selling processed books, for example, may not handle all the books the library needs; if such a supplier is used, the librarian must guard against the temptation to buy only what the supplier has available. To do so is, in effect, to allow the supplier too great an influence in library book selection.

Speed. While relative speed of receipt of books is a factor to be taken into account in comparing services, speed is sometimes given too much weight by small libraries. Certainly the library does not want to wait too long for its books, and prompt service is excellent. But all too often delay in receipt of books is the reason for reluctance to use an outside service at all. Small libraries doing their own processing can, it is true, have the best sellers on the shelves very soon after the books come; processing centers seldom provide them as quickly. On the other hand, the processing center usually receives and sends on the greater proportion of the new books long before the library itself could have managed to prepare them. The relative importance of getting the best seller into the hands of an avid reader a week or two sooner, on the one hand, and the value of adding the bulk of the books more rapidly, on the other, should be considered in relation to the library's educational objectives. Another time factor to take into account is that the outside service usually continues throughout the year without a pause, while the library's own cataloging may be held up by vacations, illnesses, and resignations.

Among the problems that will face the librarian who wishes to use a processing center are the following:

Obtaining the agreement of trustees and officials. Librarians who have wished to turn to outside processing report that it is sometimes hard to justify the cost. It is difficult for laymen to understand why cataloging and book preparation should be, as it seems to them, so expensive. A price that is low to the librarian may appear high to board members. They find it hard to comprehend what is so complicated about cataloging and classification, and why any reasonably well-educated person cannot assign call numbers and make author, title, and subject cards for books. This reaction is not surprising. It is the same as the reaction of the general public, probably including the librarian himself, at the cost of having plumbing fixed, the television set repaired, or tonsils removed. One pays for training, experience, and judgment, for the investment made in acquiring knowledge and in purchasing and keeping up to date the tools of the trade or profession. Work performed without knowledge is unsatisfactory in its results. A librarian inspecting a library cataloged and classified by an amateur can spot immediately defects that cannot fail to be reflected in poor service.

Officials and board members, even if acquainted with such tools as the *ALA Cataloging Rules for Author and Title Entries,* subject-heading books, classification schemes, and filing rules, are likely to believe that the use of such resources must be relatively simple in a small library. Some refinements and details *are* unnecessary in a small collection, but experience and judgment are required to decide which ones are needed, which not. It is particularly important, in organizing a small collection, to bring out through subject headings and call number the contents of certain books, both because the collection is small—and therefore lacks specific books in many detailed subjects—and also because the small collection does not always include the special indexes and bibliographies that would help the staff to find subject material.

Obtaining board and official approval of outside processing is more likely to be successful if considered in the context of total library planning. If community study has revealed needs that are not met and services that are not being given, the release of a sizable portion of staff time and possibly of some library space becomes meaningful in terms of what can be accomplished with this time and space. Technical processes are not an end in themselves but a means to public service. Subscribing to an outside processing service should be presented, therefore, not as an end but as a means of providing some of the public services the library has been wanting to give. Boards and officials who share the library's objectives are likely to respond favorably to a proposed change that gives the opportunity to accomplish those objectives.

Adapting the collection to the new service. Rare, indeed, is the library that receives books processed outside corresponding exactly to those previously prepared by the library's own methods. Classification of biography, location of book cards, and use of pseudonyms seem to cause the most frequent variations. In adapting to the new processing service, the librarian must look forward and not backward. As time goes on, more books and the most frequently used books will be the new ones coming in from the processing center. It is shortsighted to change the new books to fit the old; if changes are needed, they should be made to adapt existing books to the new method. But the librarian should guard against the temptation to make changes for the sake of neatness and consistency alone. Only changes that are necessary for public service should be considered, and these should be as simple as possible.

Circulation routines are probably not seriously impeded by variations in the position of book cards. Books that may be withdrawn in a year or two are certainly not worth the expense of any material change. Cross references in the catalog and shelf list may well suffice to take care of variations in entry, subject headings, and classification. Dummies on the shelves referring from the old to the new, and location symbols bringing old and new together, may be adequate in most cases to carry the library through the period of transition.

To some librarians the problems of adaptation loom so large that they seem an insuperable obstacle to the consideration of outside processing. The difficulties immediately apparent block the long view. Part of a librarian's responsibility is to look ahead, to ask what the library ought to be accomplishing in five years, in ten. If, at the cost of some temporary difficulty, the conversion to outside processing will make the library a better one in the future than it could hope to be by continuing the present method, the temporary difficulties should be accepted in the interest of long-range progress. If the librarian applies his energy and creative imagination to the problem of surmounting and minimizing the temporary difficulties, he may find them less formidable than he expected.

Adapting the staff to the new service. While in theory the librarian may have an excellent plan for utilizing the number of hours released by outside processing, he is dealing not with paper plans but with real people. How is Miss B., who has devotedly done all the cataloging for years, going to be transformed into Miss B., reference librarian, or Miss B., community worker? How is the time that the desk assistants used, between customers, for stamping, pasting, and jacketing going to be made available for the clerical work involved in the expanded service program? Librarians faced with these practical problems find little help in the surveys and studies that necessarily consider time and staff in the abstract.

Since each library's staff is different, to lay down hard and fast procedures for the change-over is impossible. The suggestions made on pages 81–82 in connection with changing staff attitudes toward public service may be helpful. Miss B.'s problem is not unique; she is, like thousands of workers, being displaced by a type of automation and needs to be trained for or oriented toward another type of library work. The fact that the process may be difficult for Miss B. and not easy for the librarian should not be a reason for failing to make the change, any more than the need to retrain and reassign workers prevents a business or industry from automating a process. In a small library, the transition is made easier by the fact that Miss B. has undoubtedly been working all along at a number of other library tasks that she knows well. The expanded program may provide opportunities for responsibilities as important as those she is relinquishing and as well suited to her talents and temperament.

Projecting and executing a major change is a task that calls for considerable administrative skill on the part of the librarian. He will probably be confronted, not only with human relations factors, but also with the need for a restudy of staff duties. The skills needed for the expanded program may be available for development in staff members who have not previously had the opportunity of serving the public. The librarian himself will undoubtedly undertake some of the new work. Taking full advantage of released time requires careful planning. Utilizing the desk assistants' time, for example, might call for a revision of circulation procedures, or for a change in the arrangement of work space near the circulation desk.

Efficient Internal Processing

If the library cannot immediately make use of outside processing, the work must continue to be done by the library staff. The librarian must wrestle with the question of the best assignment of time for processing and for direct public service, always with the long-range objectives of the library in mind. Even when outside processing is used, some processing work will still be done at the library. It behooves the librarian to make sure these tasks are done as quickly and efficiently as is consistent with the library's needs.

As in all activities in which there is routine and repetition, much can be accomplished by a serious effort toward work simplification. About each process now carried on, questions should be asked: Is this process really necessary? Is it more time-consuming than the alternative routines that would be needed if it were not done? How much does it contribute to service?

If a process is necessary, the next questions are:

Is the present method efficient?

Would a rearrangement of work space make the process easier and faster?

Is the work done by a staff member whose training and salary are appropriate for the job, or can it be done by someone with less training and skill?

Could it be broken down into several operations and performed more efficiently as a result?

Could it perhaps be done by machine?

Would different furniture and equipment improve efficiency: a lower table, more book trucks, a high stool on wheels?

As a result of asking questions like these many libraries have been able to bring about remarkable improvements. Some have abandoned long-cherished records—the accession book, for example, is rapidly vanishing from the scene. Sometimes the changes have been extremely simple: the acquisition of an adding machine, the rearrangement of a workroom, even the expenditure of a little more money for carbon paper or the relocation of a pencil sharpener. Once the staff has developed the habit of asking "why" and looking about for better ways of accomplishing work, surprising results can be obtained.

Acquisition of Materials

Most libraries that handle their own acquisitions buy new books from a jobber, a local dealer, or through publishers' representatives. The advantages of purchasing from a jobber usually include the following: a larger stock of books on hand from which orders are filled more promptly, a higher discount, and jobber's experience in selling to libraries and his familiarity with library procedures.

A local dealer offers these advantages: quick service in emergencies, opportunity to examine stock and select from it, personal service in some cases, and the intangible value of spending public funds locally. Some librarians feel that these advantages outweigh the higher discount and larger stock of the jobber. Much depends on the quality of the local service, but few local bookstores can afford to give the type of service a library needs, including supplying frequent single copies of books from publishers, making many reports, securing out-of-the-way items, and billing to meet the library's requirements. In the case of periodicals, also, most libraries find it better to place the entire subscription list in the hands of one dealer because of the larger discount gained in this way and because there is then just one source to query about nondelivery or other complications in periodical subscriptions.

The service given by jobbers varies also, and to choose a dealer, whether jobber or local store, on the basis of discount alone is a mistake. If orders are filled slowly and inaccurately, if reports are not made, if there are too many wrong editions, imperfect copies, errors in bills, and other frustrations costly in time and hampering to service, the existence of a higher discount usually does not compensate the library for its intangible losses. Often the high discount offered is misleading, and the librarian later discovers that many books are treated as exceptions and sold at list price. The dealer worth seeking and clinging to—if he can be found—offers both efficient service and a high discount.

Good service from a dealer is not a one-way street. The librarian cannot expect to receive a high discount and superior service if orders are incomplete, if titles or publishers are inaccurate or omitted, if editions are not specified. Dealers are not always responsible for delays and imperfections. The librarian must be realistic and remember that the small library's business is of less importance to the dealer, be he jobber or local bookstore owner, than that of the wholesale, multiple-copy customer on the one hand and over-the-counter sales at list price on the other. Larger libraries and cooperative systems that order jointly are in a better position, because of their larger volume of business and streamlined procedures, to bargain for service and discounts. The small library cannot expect its business to be so earnestly solicited, but it can reap the many small advantages of being a valued customer by following businesslike ordering procedures.

Although the publisher's representative is a welcome visitor in many libraries, there are dangers in too great a dependence on his services. True, he is usually well informed about the books he has to offer and often brings news of the book and library world. The danger of purchasing widely from such an agent is that he is a salesman for one publishing house. As such he cannot be expected to offer objective comparisons with the similar offerings of rivals. A persuasive salesman, as the result of one visit, can make a good portion of the budget melt away for books that may or may not be the best the library can select. Thoughtful book selection is made difficult if not impossible when many books are purchased by this method.

Experience has proved that in acquisition work, as in all processing, the exceptional routines are the most time-consuming and costly. Some exceptions are inevitable. Significant locally published books, for instance, must be obtained directly from the publisher in many cases. Careful selection sometimes makes it desirable to order a book on approval even though this procedure is costly, especially when the book must later be returned.[1]

Some libraries carry book club memberships in order to take advantage of the special prices offered. Book club choices come automatically and promptly as a rule, so that an additional saving in time and improvement in service may result. These advantages are not always unmixed blessings, however, and before initiating or continuing book club subscriptions, librarians should consider the following questions:

Are all the selections titles the library would order through its normal selection method?

Does the acceptance of the subscription, even with automatic receipt of the books, necessitate extra procedures to avoid ordering duplicates and thus offset the saving in price?

Is the book club edition satisfactory for library use as compared with the trade edition? Are its binding, paper, margins, and the like less likely to stand up under the heavy circulation that a popular book will probably have?

Answers to these questions will vary. The nature of the book club, the library's volume of orders and ordering procedures, and the amount of wear and tear on books in the community must be taken into account. If book club membership is satisfactory in most respects, a library can afford not to add the occasional unsatisfactory choice of a club normally relied on to select appropriate books. Even though some book club selections are chosen by prominent and trustworthy juries, the librarian should keep control of his collection and not automatically add any title not

---

[1] The cooperative selection arrangements described on p.102–4 make it possible for the library to see books before making a final decision to purchase.

selected according to the established policy and buying plan. In considering book club subscriptions, the library should make its decision, pro or con, after studying all the facts and should review it periodically on the basis of continued experience.

Out-of-print books constitute another exception. All libraries need titles no longer obtainable through normal channels, as publishers allow much important fiction and nonfiction no longer currently popular to go out of print. Library copies are lost or wear out, and gaps loom in the collection. A want list may be kept of such needs. It should be kept small and workable and include only important items. If a book is seldom used and if readers' requests can be satisfied by interlibrary loan, for example, a title need not be listed. Or if a nonfiction title currently available can serve satisfactorily in the place of an old stand-by, the latter need not be sought. The nonfiction titles appearing most frequently on want lists are those needed because they are indexed in some reference source or because they contain hard-to-find information frequently called for.

Checking out-of-print catalogs against a want list is time-consuming and not always rewarding. Experience will indicate which dealer's lists are likely to contain valuable titles. In exceptional cases a library may advertise for a badly needed item, or a list of important needs be given to a qualified secondhand book dealer, with a request for quotations as the books become available. The problem of out-of-print titles can also be approached from another angle. The Reprint Expediting Service of the American Library Association is interested in being informed of out-of-print books needed by libraries and is sometimes successful in persuading publishers to reissue them. If the library has a microfilm reader, the purchase of a film of an important out-of-print book of nonfiction used frequently for reference purposes (for example, a county history) may be a partial solution.

At best, exceptional book ordering is unsatisfactory for the small library and provides another instance where a system or cooperative ordering arrangement may have certain advantages. When the ordering of several libraries is pooled, the exceptions for the individual small library can be considered normal routines for the larger operation and thus become more manageable. For example, the combining of want lists, against which dealers' lists of out-of-print books can be checked once for all libraries, is more efficient than separate searching by each library.

Ordering Procedure, Receiving Books, and Paying Bills

The essential element of the book order, for the dealer, is the accurate indication of what the library wants. For the library, it is the record that tells: what is on order—to be checked against books received and to avoid unwanted duplication; the dealer to whom each order has been sent; and the date of each order, so that older orders may be checked or canceled.

Many libraries find that a multiple order form is best adapted to these purposes. Its various parts can be used as:

The order itself. When sent to the dealer, he can use it in any way that fits his procedures: file by title or publisher, hold for delayed orders, and so on

The record of the order in the library's alphabetical file. If the slip contains the name of the dealer (or, if the library has one regular dealer, only the names of the occasional exceptions) and the date of the order, such a record fills the library's needs reasonably well

A form for purchasing catalog cards for the book ordered

Some libraries use additional carbons for such purposes as: a work slip on which the cataloger prepares copy for the typist; a temporary entry in the catalog, to inform the public that a book is on order (this form is removed when the regular card is filed); and a record in a chronological file prepared by date of order, to facilitate checking on back orders. These extra uses entail additional work. To decide whether this work is justified, each library should apply the test question: Does the improvement in efficiency or service justify the time diverted from other tasks? The answer will vary from library to library.

When books are received from a dealer, it is necessary to open the boxes and check immediately to determine: (1) whether the box contains the books listed on the invoice (the list enclosed which is supposed to correspond with the box's contents) and (2) whether the books are the ones actually ordered by the library. Obvious imperfections should also be noted at this time, but most libraries have abandoned the practice of page-by-page inspection as too costly. These operations should be performed before any stamping of ownership, marking, or pasting is done.

Dealers' bills should be paid as promptly as possible. Sometimes the bill is identical with the invoice—that is, a copy of the former has been used to supply the latter. If not, the bill must be checked against the invoice, to ensure that the library is being billed only for books actually received. Needless to say, no library pays for a book until it has been received either by the library itself or by the processing center authorized to receive it. Occasionally there may be an exception to this rule, as when a subscription to an important set of books is paid in advance because it can be ordered in no other way. Such exceptions should be kept to a minimum and made only when the publisher or dealer involved is known to be reliable.

Working with a Purchasing Department

Libraries whose acquisition and ordering procedures are subject to the review of a purchasing agent or department may encounter special problems. Purchasing departments are sometimes bound by official regulations or ordinances and may follow such procedures as:

Offering the library's entire book or periodical purchasing contract to the lowest bidder on a competitive basis. Occasionally a library goes through the harrowing process of changing dealers fairly frequently because of this practice and may have to revamp its procedures to fit each new dealer's methods. Discount is not by any means an infallible guide to the best dealer. If possible, librarians faced with this situation should work out, perhaps with the cooperation of the purchasing department, standards of service to be required of all bidders for the contract. Dealers known through experience to fall short of the standards can be disqualified, and those found to give substandard service can be dropped for failing to meet specifications

Requiring a list of book orders in sheet form. Purchasing departments which keep a file of all official orders may not wish to file multiple order slips. Orders in sheet form are not usually so efficient for the library, and if possible some compromise should be worked out that will enable the library to use the method best adapted to its own operation. Perhaps the needs of the purchasing department can be met with a sheet bearing the order number, dealer, date, number of items ordered, and total cost— with the understanding, of course, that the complete information is available at the library

Deferring the payment of bills. If, as is generally done, each group of books ordered from one dealer at one time is considered one order and given one order number, some purchasing department policies create problems when orders are only partially filled. A policy sometimes exists of paying only for completed orders—a practice which seems reasonable to the officials concerned, but works a hardship on the library and dealer alike. Books go out of stock, publication dates are postponed, and dealers cannot complete orders. Even though they promptly supply the majority of the items, it may be months before they can send the few missing ones.

If the purchasing department does not pay the bill, even though the library has long ago received most of the books, the library's credit relations with the dealer may become strained. The library's financial records are also affected. For example, if there is an incomplete order toward the end of the budget year, the librarian is confronted with a dilemma. If he assumes the bill will be paid before the end of the year and guesses wrong, he will finish the year with an unspent balance in his book budget, sorely needed for other books. If he takes the chance that the bill will not be paid until next year and guesses wrong, he is overspent. Since either of these situations is serious, most librarians resolve the dilemma by canceling the unfilled orders so that the bill may be paid and reordering the books later. This time-wasting operation may sometimes be avoided if the situation is understood by the purchasing official.

Purchasing rules, in general, are made to fit the normal purchases of a jurisdiction, which usually include either large separate items or multiple or bulk goods. The library's order for fifty separate books is different from the health department's order for fifty identical rolls of adhesive tape, and a good purchasing agent will understand the difference and make what compromises he can in his procedures in the interest of library efficiency

Cataloging and Classification

Even if the library cannot avail itself of complete outside processing services, it can obtain help in cataloging and classification from one or more of the following sources: printed cards purchased from the Library of Congress or the H. W. Wilson Company for nonfiction titles;[2] entries in the "Weekly Record" section of *Publishers' Weekly,* cumulated in the *American Book Publishing Record Annual Index;* and entries in the American Library Association *Booklist* and in the Wilson catalogs.

Adaptations may be needed on occasion but should be kept to a minimum. Normally changes will be made only in the direction of simplification. Call numbers, for example, may be shortened in some cases. If the library's catalog has been under the care of an older, perfectionist cataloger, the library's existing cataloging may reflect practices no longer used even in large libraries. For instance, the painstaking search for the real names of pseudonymous authors is a thing of the past in most libraries. Books are entered under the name on the title page as a rule, with cross references to other names used by the same author when known. Middle names, dates, and other identifications are not searched, unless there is a genuine possibility of confusion among authors represented in the library's own catalog. Identification by size is needed in the small library only for oversize books that are separately shelved.

Simplification is desirable only to the extent that it meets the library's needs. If eliminating the date of publication from cards for fiction means double searching when a review is sought, the date may be worth noting should the library be asked for many reviews of novels. If noting an illustration saves searching through a number of pictureless biographies for a portrait, the note may be worth making. Listing of contents, as in collections of plays, may save effort in the long run, if the library does not have published indexes to plays. Decisions of this type should be made as a general policy which is written down and followed regularly, and not on the basis of each individual book. The policy should be reviewed at intervals, to make sure the library

---

[2] Wilson cards (in sets only) may be ordered with or without call numbers and subject headings in place on the cards. They may be paid for by coupon, a simple method preferred by many small libraries. Lists of cards available are sent monthly to libraries that use the service. Full information may be obtained from the H. W. Wilson Company. Library of Congress cards may be purchased individually. Call numbers and subject headings are traced at the bottom of cards, but not printed or typed at the top, when sets are ordered. Information on ordering and payment may be obtained from the Card Division of the Library of Congress.

is not blindly following traditional procedures which no longer serve a useful purpose.

Cataloging policy should take into account anticipated growth in the library's collection. It is costly and inefficient to make cards so simple and call numbers so short that they will soon become inadequate. If areas in the collection are rapidly expanding, class numbers may need to be carried a place or two further to avoid too many books in one class, with resulting problems of location and shelving. If the library has been using only class numbers, it may be desirable to begin identifying books further by adding the author's last name or initial to the call number. New books may be identified in this way without affecting their relationship with the older ones, and shelving and book location are made easier. Not every small library will need this step; whether it is worth considering will depend on the size of the total collection and the number of volumes with the same class number. The use of the author's last name or initial is preferred to the use of Cutter numbers by many small libraries.

If the librarian has any reason to believe that the library may later become a member of a processing center, or receive processed books from an outside source, he will be wise to find out what decisions have been made at the center or commercial source and consider adapting to them, always with the understanding that adaptation does not mean changing the entire existing collection. As in the case of the member library, it is much better to accept future practices as the library's standard, now, rather than to plan to continue to make small changes in new books received from outside.

The library that does its own cataloging should keep its catalog procedures, as well as its policy, simple and efficient. For example, it is wise to have one staff member in charge of the catalog. Even though the actual work may be shared, it is less likely to suffer from neglect and inconsistency if one person is given the final responsibility. If feasible, time for catalog work should be scheduled, to avoid the piling up of a backlog. More and better work can be accomplished if it can be done in quiet times while the library is closed or in an area away from the public, rather than at odd moments between customers. Of course, if the library's staffing pattern requires that some cataloging be taken to a public desk, public service must be given priority, and the cataloger must guard against showing or feeling annoyance when a reader approaches.

A record of major cataloging and classification decisions should be kept by the library that has not entrusted its catalog work to a processing center. Catalogers do leave or retire, taking with them a wealth of accumulated knowledge and experience. While not all this wisdom can be set down on paper, a brief record of what has been decided, and why, can ease the life of the successor. The library that has proudly depended on Miss X.'s remarkable memory is in trouble when Miss X. is gone.

Preparing New Books for Use

Book preparation requires considerable handling, no matter what the system. It is an area which especially repays study leading toward simplification. A specific work space and the use of a number of simple devices can speed up work greatly. If possible, books should move from work station to work station on an assembly-line basis, even if each station cannot be manned at the same time. Removal of books from tables to trucks and back to tables is wasteful and should be eliminated. If work space prohibits assembly-line layout, however, the use of trucks is certainly preferable to the practice of hand-carrying loads of books from one point to another. Even in larger systems and processing centers, the preparation of books is partially a volume-by-volume operation, in contrast to card production which can be more completely mechanized. In the larger unit, book cards and pockets can be machine duplicated, and the use of pasting machines and a carefully planned layout may result in economies beyond the reach of the smaller library.

Routines connected with making books ready for the shelves vary according to the library's practice. Probably the most important variation involves plastic jackets. Few changes affecting the library world have created more discussion. On the favorable side these arguments are advanced:

Jackets are attractive. They lead readers to books
They prolong the life of a book, postponing and sometimes eliminating the expense of rebinding
They brighten the appearance of the library
It is an advantage to have the blurb and biographical sketch automatically attached to the book

The opposition can marshal an equally impressive set of arguments. They include the following:

Jackets used on books are not available for displays

Plastic jackets, if improperly attached, may obscure important endpapers

Some readers and librarians dislike the feel of plastic covers

Some librarians prefer their libraries to present a dignified appearance. They believe jackets add an unseemly commercial note

The cost of the jackets themselves, along with the time spent putting them on, is felt by some to be too high. They prefer to spend the money for more books and use the time for other services

In some communities mutilation of the cheaper sorts of jackets is a problem. Children especially are prone to tear plastic covers

If librarians and readers like plastic jackets, many of the above objections can be countered. Additional book jackets can be obtained from publishers for promotional purposes, plastic jackets are often put on books as an automatic part of a processing service, and the newer Mylar jackets are almost indestructible.

When the decision has been made to use or not to use plastic jackets, other aspects of preparing books for use can be decided. If jackets are used, it is not always necessary to mark call numbers on the spines of the new volumes themselves as well as on the jackets, since in many cases the jacket will remain until the book is ready to be withdrawn. The call number can be marked on the jacket itself, if appropriate, or can be typed or lettered on a sticker which is affixed to the jacket. Some librarians prefer to have the call numbers placed on both the jacket and the spine of the book so that, when the jacket is lost or worn-out, the book needs no additional processing before circulation.

Marks of ownership need not be complicated. The name of the library stamped in large letters across the top leaves of the book, or the lower leaves if the top ones are stained, is now usually considered sufficient. Libraries using plastic jackets often place under the transparent cover a printed slip proclaiming ownership. Embossing and secret markings on special pages are no longer considered worth the cost.

Another relic of bygone days rapidly becoming extinct is the careful opening of each book, page by page. This treatment was supposed to prevent the premature breaking of the book's back and probably did prevent damage in some cases. But the job was a time-consuming one and is no longer considered worth the effort in the average public library.

If call numbers are to be placed on the book spines, this may be done by hand in libraries where the staff includes a letterer who can work with ink or an automatic stylus fast and neatly. More usually numbers are typed on adhesive-backed paper labels and attached to the spine; a coating of shellac helps make the attachment more permanent.[3] Various new means of numbering spines are being tried, such as pressure transfers and heat-fusing plastics, and may prove to be practical.

Many libraries separate on the shelves such popular types of fiction as mysteries, westerns, and science fiction. Stickers indicating these categories can be purchased from suppliers and are easily affixed.

The preparation of books for use depends on the circulation system. Book cards and pockets must be typed and the pockets and date due slips pasted in, if they are used. Should the volume of work warrant, a pasting machine is helpful. If the library is a rural one with a number of small outlets using a fluid collection, location file cards must also be made.

Binding, Mending, Withdrawing, Replacing

When a book is in poor physical condition, the library is faced with decisions on two levels. The first is professional and has to do with the importance of the book to the collection. It involves determining whether the book should be kept at all: whether it has been superseded by other titles, whether its popularity has waned, whether there are enough copies still in the library, and whether its availability through interlibrary loan or cooperative arrangement will suffice.

If the book is important enough to keep, the second decision— this time a technical one—needs to be made. Can and should the book be rebound, should it be mended, or should a new copy be ordered? In the early days of public libraries, when salaries were so low that many who worked in libraries were almost volunteers, the relative value of books and of staff time was markedly different from the situation today. It was then worthwhile to devote hours to the mending of books in order to preserve them, even when replacement copies could be purchased. Occasionally a library still follows this practice, with questionable economy.

[3] For information about adhesives, see Gladys Piez, "Some Library Adhesives—A Laboratory Evaluation of P.V.A.'s," *ALA Bulletin,* 56:838–43 (October, 1962).

The degree of damage to the book is the determining factor in making the decision as to whether to mend, rebind, or replace. If one page is torn, a simple mending operation will take care of it. Library mending is a skill to be learned, and library supply houses have developed materials and adhesives especially adapted to library use. It is scarcely necessary to warn against the use of any transparent tape other than the mending tape obtained from library suppliers. Supply houses sometimes offer instruction in simple mending to groups of staff members from neighboring libraries.

Another situation in which mending may be required occurs when an important and unobtainable book has become worn and cannot be rebound. For example, local history, a biography of local significance, may already have been rebound and yet need further attention. Its paper may be so brittle that further rebinding is impossible. In such cases, careful mending may be justified.

Normally, however, mending should be kept to a minimum. If a book is worth keeping, it should usually be replaced or rebound. Which procedure to follow will depend on several factors. A rebinding is normally sturdier than the trade binding and therefore more satisfactory if hard wear is anticipated. On the other hand, rebound books may be less inviting in appearance than new ones and their inner margins decreased so that reading becomes difficult. The cost of good library binding is not low; it sometimes approaches the original cost of the book itself.

If books are dirty, if pages are marked, rebinding with a bright new cover will not improve the inside appearance. Children's books, in particular, receive hard wear and are subject to all sorts of hazards from crayon drawings to sticky finger marks. Rebinding these is obviously less satisfactory than replacing them.

Children's books are available to libraries in prebound form, which prolongs their life considerably. As the original cost is higher, the added period of usefulness must be great enough to compensate for it. Not all children's books are purchased prebound since some librarians find that, while the binding remains strong for a long time, the inside pages become torn and grimy fairly soon. In such cases, it is better to purchase and replace in the publisher's binding. Community habits, number of children, and age for which a book is written are factors that help the librarian make this decision. Some publishers' bindings for children's books are quite strong, approaching the quality of pre-binding.[4]

Larger libraries that do considerable reference work ordinarily bind periodical volumes, but smaller libraries frequently do not. The cost of this type of binding is high. Small libraries are more likely to circulate their back issues of magazines and thus do not wish to bind them.

If a small library is actively engaged in reference work, has space to keep back files, and frequently uses periodical indexes, some form of periodical binding may be worth considering, particularly if a cooperative arrangement among a number of smaller libraries results in their sharing responsibility for keeping back files of different periodicals. Other methods of storing and preserving older periodicals are not very satisfactory. Pamphlet boxes with or without lids, flat shelving, tying up in various ways—all these devices and methods are cumbersome, especially for reshelving or replacing magazines that have been used.

Inventory

Many small libraries take annual inventories—a practice impossible for most larger libraries because of the cost involved. Such frequent inventories may not be justified by results. Normally the librarian who works closely with the collection becomes aware of missing books without a formal inventory, and can check to make sure they are gone before removing cards or ordering replacements. Unlocated reserves also bring to light missing volumes. If the library has the misfortune to lose a great many books through direct theft rather than through the circulation process, an inventory may be needed. In such a case, measures to control future unauthorized "borrowing" should be considered.

Inventory is also probably needed in the library that has grown haphazardly without proper organization. If, for example, a new librarian finds books on the shelves that do not appear in the catalog, as well as many cards in the catalog for which there are apparently no books, fairly drastic measures are necessary and an inventory may have to be taken. In general, however, the librarian should carefully weigh the value of frequent inventories against the cost in staff time and disruption to service.

[4] "Publishers' Library Bindings," *Library Journal*, 87:1661–65 (April 15, 1962).

Circulation

Modern thinking about circulation routines attempts to reduce work to minimum essentials. Librarians used to think it necessary to be able to locate every book at any moment, to know how many times each volume had circulated, to retrieve overdue books at all costs, and to count circulation by classification. Registration files by name and number were painstakingly kept up to date, with many hours devoted to changing addresses and names.

In view of the rising costs of personnel, most libraries have abandoned all or at least some of these facets of circulation work. While some loss has been entailed, not only in books but in possibly useful information, a comparison of that loss with the cost of avoiding it has weighed the balance in favor of the simpler systems and against the older concept of the complex, all-embracing record. Larger libraries, whose costs are high, have been among the first to make changes; some small libraries still cling to the old ways.

A circulation system must provide the following information:

Who has a given book that is overdue?
When was it due?
What specific books have been lost in circulation and must be withdrawn from the library's records?

These are the essentials. Normally a library wants to know also how many books it has circulated, and most charging systems provide that information, although many of the new ones provide for no further breakdown.

If libraries, through some miraculous device, could know in advance which books would be returned on time, no records would need to be made for such circulation. A simple count would suffice. Since books returned without any prodding are fortunately in the majority, most circulation work is actually done for the exceptional case. The realization that libraries record all circulation chiefly in order to be able to trace the relatively small proportion of the total that become overdue may come as a shock to some. In practice, the keeping of the record probably acts as a deterrent to prevent theft and failure to return books and also affords subsidiary benefits, such as a complete record of transactions, making reserve and inventory work easier.

Any large-scale routine that consumes considerable time ought to be kept as simple as possible. Circulation studies have therefore been made, and libraries have streamlined procedures. Some have abandoned registration files altogether; many have given up the numerical file. Under some systems, much of the work formerly done by the staff is now done by the reader himself; while this does save staff time, the loss of the reader's time must be considered in weighing the advantages of such a system. Slipping of returned books is unnecessary in many of the new systems, and prestamped date-due slips have replaced the stamping of dates in the book itself. Some libraries have converted their systems to one loan period, and some have taken the additional step of making all books due on a given day of the week.

In deciding what circulation system to adopt or whether to make a change, the small library must consider the same factors as the large one. What does it want to find out? How much effort and expense is this information worth? The local situation must be taken into account, also. What is the volume of circulation, the cost of installation of the new system? What are the habits of readers—are they law-abiding individuals who can be depended upon to return their library books? Do they normally borrow many books at a time, so that a system which turns over much of the work to the borrower would cause resentment and create a serious public relations problem? Do the readers reserve a great many books, so that problems of location under a new system must be considered?

The search for economy in a circulation system should not, of course, blind the librarian to the service aspects of his decision. It is excellent to be able to perform the essential routines faster and better, especially if the time saved can go into other library services. But all economies that restrict service in any way should be scrutinized with great care; unless they are balanced by valid service improvements made possible by time released through the streamlining of routines, such restrictive economies can be justified only when the library is forced by a financial crisis to make them.

While important studies have been made of existing systems, with recommendations for libraries of various sizes, the ideal circulation system has not yet been devised. When it comes, it may not be suitable for the small library. Nevertheless, this is an area in which new developments are constantly appearing.

The librarian finds it difficult to know when to act and when to wait for another and better system to come into being.

If the librarian and the board agree that a library must have a new system, the various existing ones should first be studied. Libraries using them should be visited, if possible, for observation. Expert-written studies will, of course, be given special attention. A new system ought to provide accuracy and simplicity. If the library's circulation warrants, the borrower's name and address should appear on the circulation record itself, and thus do away with the necessity for registration files. Delinquent files will probably be necessary, but a library should seriously question whether an alphabetical file of total registration is needed. This loosening of the controls seems like unpardonable laxity to some; whether it is workable will depend on the habits of the community.

A new system should, if volume of circulation warrants, save time at the point of return. If books can go at once to the shelves when readers return them, the effect is almost like an increase in book budget. A considerable number of books are immediately available for readers—books in demand, at that— that would not have been on the shelves under a system that held them behind a desk for some time. If, as is likely, the new system does not allow analysis of circulation by type or classification, occasional spot checks can provide a fairly accurate approximation of an actual count. Even these samplings should be taken only if the information is essential to the library.

If the library decides to wait, in the hope that someone will devise *the* circulation system in the near future, it can still take steps to streamline the present one. Is it sending more notices per book than are necessary? Can it use date-due slips? Can existing procedures be improved by a time-and-motion study or by a change in locations and work space? Is more checking being done than is justified by the number of errors found? Consideration of these and similar questions will help the library operation now, and will also assist in setting the stage for any new system to be adopted later.

In circulation as in book processing, exceptions to the general rule are costly. Some exceptions become necessary as the library's service is enriched. Films, for example, must circulate for a very short loan period if the library's investment in film circuit membership is to be realized in service. Recordings as well as films must be inspected for damage after circulation if possible. The circulation of rental books constitutes another exception. Some libraries have reduced special procedures for rentals to a minimum by charging a fixed rental, paid at the time the book circulates. The payment entitles the borrower to keep the book for the regular loan period for free books, after which regular fines accrue. This procedure has the advantage of warning the borrower that he is taking a rental book at the outset and also makes unnecessary special rental computers.

Whenever feasible, however, circulation routines should be standardized. If the library's book collection is large enough, a single, longer loan period for all books, without renewals, saves staff time and permits the use of simpler equipment with some mechanical charging systems.

Technical Processes and Public Relations

Explaining the importance of technical functions to laymen—trustees, appropriating officials, and others—is sometimes difficult. What is done behind the scenes is always less obviously necessary to the consumer, whether he is shopping at a supermarket, buying gas at a service station, or borrowing a book from the library. To interpret the value of these unsuspected, and therefore often unappreciated, activities is not the least important of the many duties of the busy librarian of the small library.

The librarian is more likely to convince others if he is convinced himself. First of all, he must be sure that his time budget is in balance: that service needs are kept in mind and that technical processes are given enough attention to improve service, but not enough to stifle it. Secondly, he must be sure that he is on solid ground when any detail or aspect of the technical work is questioned. Is the work really streamlined as much as it might be? In thinking through the routines, in asking "Why," he will often discover the answers to give inquirers who find it difficult to understand why the staff must sometimes work away from the public, why a clerk cannot catalog the new books, why so many staff members are needed in a library, and what the staff is doing on duty when the library itself is closed. If the librarian succeeds in getting his message understood, he will have explained not only the need for technical processes, but also the purpose and philosophy of the public library itself.

Bibliography

Duchac, Kenneth. "Streamlining the Catalog," *I.L.A. Record*, 6:87–88 (June, 1953).

Frieze, William S. "The Administrator Looks at Technical Processing: The Public Library," *Library Resources and Technical Services*, 1:203–6 (Fall, 1957).

MacQuarrie, Catherine. "Cost Survey: Cost of Ordering, Cataloging and Preparations in Southern California Libraries," *Library Resources and Technical Services*, 6:337–50 (Fall, 1962).

Marvin, James C. "Technical Services—Target or Taurus," *Missouri Library Association Quarterly*, 22:37–42 (June, 1961).

Piercy, Esther J. "Cost, Time and Terms," *Library Resources and Technical Services*, 6:336 (Fall, 1962).

———— "Organization and Control of Materials," in Roberta Bowler, ed., *Local Public Library Administration*, p.195–240. Chicago: International City Managers' Assn., 1964.

Wheeler, Joseph L. "Streamlining Technical Processes in Small Libraries," *Wilson Library Bulletin*, 28:422–24 (January, 1954).

———— "Work Simplification in Libraries," *Public Libraries*, 6:14–18 (April, 1952).

Centralized Processing

Bendix, Dorothy. "Regional Processing in Public Libraries: A Survey," *Library Resources and Technical Services*, 2:155–70 (Summer, 1958).

Bundy, Mary Lee. "Behind Central Processing," *Library Journal*, 88:3539–43 (October 1, 1963).

Dennis, Willard K. "Too Soon Oldt and Too Late Schmardt," *Oklahoma Librarian*, 9:4–5 (January, 1959).

Eckford, Mary Lathrop. "The Library Service Center of Eastern Ohio: An Experience in Centralized Processing," *Library Resources and Technical Services*, 5:5–33 (Winter, 1961).

Kenney, Brigitte L. *Cooperative Centralized Processing: A Report of the Establishment and First Year of Operation of the Southwest Missouri Library Service, Inc.* Chicago: A.L.A., 1959. 98p.

Mahoney, Orcena. "Centralized Cataloging, Development and Problems," *Oklahoma Librarian*, 6:80–81 (October, 1956).

———— "Centralized Processing Centers," *Library Resources and Technical Services*, 5:40–46 (Winter, 1961).

Circulation

Fry, George, and Associates, Inc. *Study of Circulation Control Systems.* Chicago: A.L.A., 1961. 138p.

Geer, Helen T. *Charging Systems.* Chicago: A.L.A., 1955. 177p.

Kaiser, Walter H. "Are Registrations and Library Cards Musts?" *Library Journal,* 82:1393–99 (June 1, 1957).

Mallison, Glenn. "A Nonmechanical System for Sorting and Retrieving Book Cards," *Wilson Library Bulletin,* 33:362–63 (January 1, 1959).

8

BUILDING, FURNITURE, EQUIPMENT, SUPPLIES

The setting in which library service is given contributes much to the service itself. First of all, an attractive library is an inducement to library use. Secondly, a library that is easy to find, simple to use, and efficient in its layout, makes possible effective utilization of its resources by public and staff alike. In addition, a library that combines attractiveness with functional efficiency creates for itself an image that is subtly, but quite definitely, different from that created by an unattractive and inefficient building. Many a library has moved from one building to another, taking the same books and the same staff, and found that its prestige in the community has risen remarkably simply because the public has judged the product by the package.

The Library Building

Unless the library is fortunate enough to have a building that is large enough, functional, and physically attractive, the librarian and trustees should do whatever is possible to achieve a more effective setting for library service. Possibilities will vary: a new building, remodeling and enlargement of the existing structure, or refurbishing and improving of the present building without further construction.

Many of the details of library construction are beyond the scope of a book such as this one. A multiplicity of decisions about building materials, heating and air conditioning, wiring, and floor covering must be made when the library is being remodeled or rebuilt. Expert advice from architect and contractor is essential. This chapter will deal primarily with those general considerations about a building which call for knowledge the librarian himself is best able to supply.

156

Many small library buildings in the United States date back to the time when Andrew Carnegie's philanthropy gave its great impetus to the public library movement. These buildings have served their communities well, but population patterns and library service trends have changed. The time has come, in many communities, to leave an old and much-loved building for a more suitable one.

To Remodel or To Rebuild?

The cost of a new library building is high for a small community, and the first impulse of citizens and trustees alike is often to enlarge the present one. Successful remodelings of Carnegie buildings, or others of the same era, have been accomplished in some places, but often the cost is little less than that of a completely new structure. Remodeling should not be considered if the library is poorly situated, or if it is so constructed that the new layout cannot be functional—if, for example, the remodeling breaks the area for public use into several small rooms, presenting problems of supervision.

Before the decision to remodel is irrevocably made, trustees and prominent citizens should see slides and pictures of new library buildings or, if possible, the buildings themselves. The impact of such a viewing, the pleasure and excitement that arise with the prospect of a completely new and different library setting, are often the beginning of a successful building campaign and a new concept of library service as a whole.

Planning a New Building

If a new library building is decided upon, a major decision has been made, but even more important ones are to follow. The library is at a turning point in its history, and wisdom and judgment of a high order are called for. Two kinds of judgment are needed: that which comes from within, from knowledge of the library's program and activities and the particular community it serves; and that which comes from without—the know-how of the building expert.

If possible, a good architect should be employed. Economy is sometimes urged as a reason for avoiding architect's fees, but here, as elsewhere, "economy" is a word that has long-range as well as immediate meaning. Where is the economy in saving a relatively small sum in so important a venture as a new building if thereby the library is to be poorly planned, nonfunctional, and aesthetically unsatisfactory? While an architect is necessary, however, it is unrealistic to expect him to be a library expert. Some aspects of the planning of a new library building only a librarian understands. An architect is not likely to know how much space is needed for a workroom, for example, or how large a children's room should be.

Working with an architect in planning a library building is an experience that comes only once or not at all to most librarians. Because of this, another expert, such as the director of a large library with a number of branches, is usually called in as a librarian consultant. Such a consultant can be invaluable in contributing information about building plans that have been successful in other places and in evaluating the practicality of proposals for the building being considered. If the budget does not permit employing such a person in addition to the architect, the state library agency may be able to help.

Even with these experts to assist, the librarian and trustees must make many decisions. Reading articles in library and architectural journals; observing with a newly aware eye the arrangements, materials, and furnishings of all kinds of buildings, from banks to drive-ins; scrutinizing the library service not as it is but as it might be—these become important activities for the librarian, board, and staff.

The new look at the library's operation is most significant. Those who work in older and crowded library buildings are not always aware how much of their activity is shaped by their environment. For example, librarians often underestimate needed workroom space because adaptation to crowded working conditions has become so much second nature to them that a little more work space seems enormous. The use pattern of the old building is also a dangerous guide. If there seems to be a tendency for people to take books home rather than work in the library, is it because space is inadequate, the lighting poor, or the library noisy, with insufficient separation of age groups and intolerable study conditions? If these circumstances were changed, might not people's habits of use change also? Has the library perhaps adapted to these problems by circulating many books normally kept for reference use? If so, the librarian must be on guard to allow adequate space for seating and for the reference collection in the new building.

These are common examples of pitfalls in planning; others,

less obvious, could be cited. Sometimes a sacrifice is called for, as when one of the librarian's most cherished ideas, which was a brilliant adaptation to the old conditions, turns out to be inappropriate to a new building. Soul-searching and imagination are essential. The librarian must ask, "Do we do it this way because we must in this building, or because in any building this way is best?"

This is the time to ask long-range questions: Is there a possibility that we may cooperate with another library or system for a part of our service or activity? Will we join a processing center and therefore need much less space for book preparation activities? Will our storage needs be affected by an arrangement whereby we can command unusual books quickly from another library? Will we need to plan for a recordings collection, now or in the future? Will we be likely ever to have a branch or a bookmobile and therefore need to plan to add facilities for loading and shipping?

Choosing a Site

The future of the library is bound up with the future of the community; this is true of all library activities, but especially so in building plans. A new building will be expected to serve for a long time. How large will the community be in ten years? in twenty? Projected growths are available to help here. In which direction is the community growing, and where will business and shopping activities be centered as growth occurs? The chamber of commerce and local or state planners will have some answers. An attractive and relatively new library building left behind by the growth of a community, or stranded on a back street because a wrong guess was made or a short-sighted decision adopted, is a sad sight.

If a compromise must be made between a good, smaller site and a larger, but poorly located one, many librarians would choose the former as the lesser evil. Officials are sometimes reluctant to pay the cost of a good location. "If people want to use the library, they'll find it," is a frequent argument—right up to a point, but only in part. The population of any community includes a number of people who will seek out the library and use it at whatever difficulty and inconvenience to themselves. This proportion will vary with the nature of the community, but it is never large. There is also a group of the opposite type—those who will not use the library even if it is next door. This, too, is fortunately usually a small fragment of the total population. The largest group is composed of those who fall between these two extremes. The library provided for their use, and for which they help to pay, can and frequently will become a vital part of their lives if it is easy to reach and constantly called to their attention by its proximity to shopping and other areas they visit often.

Planners and other officials often think of a library as a handsome and appropriate addition to a group of other civic buildings. Such combinations, if planned and harmonious, are usually an attractive sight; they give people a sense of pride in their community; and they make convenient such official occasions as budget presentations and other necessary conferences of the official family. But is a city hall, a county courthouse, or even a museum or municipal auditorium the best neighbor for a public library that should—if the community is to realize to the fullest the value of its investment in books, staff, and building—be a busy place visited by large numbers of people? The answer is not always no, but it frequently is. Those responsible for site selection must ask, first and insistently, what else there is in the neighborhood that draws people frequently and regularly—people of all ages and kinds whom the library is, or ought to be, equipped to serve.

In site selection, as in building planning, the librarian should not rely too much on present use. If the present building is used heavily by children but not by adults, the site may be the reason. A new site is sometimes selected in a park near a playground because it is ideal for children, it provides a pleasing setting for an attractive building, and it has the added advantage of saving money another site would cost, since the community already owns the park site. The result is often a bigger and better children's library, giving excellent service to the community's youth, but failing in its obligation to serve adults as well.

Refurbishing the Existing Building

Not every librarian can have a new building, at least not immediately. Every librarian, however, can make sure the building in which he operates is as attractive and efficient as possible. If the building is an old and familiar one, perhaps he does not really see it as it would appear to a newcomer. Shabbiness, inconveniences, crowded conditions, may be accepted and go practically unnoticed by him.

The first step, then, toward improving a library's appearance and efficiency is to stand back and take a long, hard look at it. From the outside, is it obvious to all passers-by that this *is* a library? If not, a clear and attractive sign is needed. If the building is set back from the sidewalk and partly obscured by trees in summer, the sign may be needed at the front of the lot, rather than on the building itself. And if the library is located on a quiet side street, signs several blocks away—on the principal surrounding streets—should point to the existence and location of the public library.

What can be done to improve the outside of the building depends on the style of architecture, the building material, and the nature of the community. Paint will help some buildings, a clean-up job others. If there are grass and shrubs, they should be well cared for. Replacement of an old-fashioned entrance with a modern one is effective, if money can be found for such an improvement. A new and lighter door to replace a heavy one is a boon to children and older people, since fire regulations usually require that doors open outward. Windows should be clean and should open and close with ease.

What impression does the inside of the library building give a newcomer? Many a library is dark and gloomy, with a musty, institutional smell. New lighting may be needed to facilitate reading and finding books. In many older libraries the furniture and woodwork are dark and massive. The loan desk, in particular, is often cumbersome and so placed that it is the first thing a patron sees on entering. Moving the loan desk to one side of the entrance, or, better still, replacing it with a modern one less centrally located, will often create a sense of space as well as a much more welcoming atmosphere. Painting woodwork and walls a lighter color lightens and brightens a building, and if furniture cannot be replaced, it too may benefit from a paint job.

Most people enter the library to find books, and the librarian looking critically at his building must ask whether they can find what they want easily. Are directional signs clean and clear? Do they say what they mean in words the reader can understand, or do they perhaps point to the "900's" instead of to "Travel" and "History," or to the "Charging Desk"—a term many readers do not understand? Perhaps the books have been shifted but not the shelf labels, or the cards moved in the catalog but not the tray labels. The catalog should be marked and have nearby a clear guide to its use, again couched in plain English and not in library jargon. If there are stacks or alcoves, signs should help the reader find his way to the book he wants, and he should not have to ask where to register, where to return books, or where to go for information. If the books are so tightly shelved that they are hard to remove, or if the shelves themselves are so high that the top one cannot be reached, the library needs more shelving, more space—or a good weeding. The reader's comfort as well as his convenience should be considered. Space to write and study should be available, as well as a few comfortable chairs for those browsing for pleasure.

Familiar objects, such as old pictures, statuary, and other museum pieces, may have had their day. Replacing the sepia engravings with attractive and colorful pictures (perhaps received as gifts or on loan from the local art museum) and the stuffed owls with flower arrangements provided by the garden club will work a remarkable transformation. An attractive screen might close off a corner necessarily used for work space, an old and unused fireplace be covered over, a rearrangement of standing shelves and tables provide more space, and appropriate curtains give a softer touch to an overaustere interior. Many of these changes can be accomplished with little expense, if imagination is used.

A Second Service Outlet

Libraries called "small" by the Preface definition—that is, those with not more than three professional staff members—usually have neither the need nor the ability to establish a branch. However, public demand may call for another outlet, or unusual circumstances may justify considering one. The community may have grown in one direction, so that most of the population lives in a new area some distance from the old center where the library is located. A new outlying shopping center may attract many residents away from the old shopping district. In some cases, the best plan might be removal of the library to the new shopping area, but more often service is still needed in the older area, and the librarian and board may have to give serious thought to a new outlet for outlying residents. Other circumstances making advisable the consideration of a new outlet may be the opening of a superhighway that cuts off half the people from easy access to the library, or the annexation of a new area. The small rural or county library is, of course, quite different from the library serving a compact community and usually requires several service points.

Library service may be supplied to a new area in several ways. One solution, not often the first to be considered, may be the simplest and best—cooperation or agreement with a neighboring jurisdiction to give library service to the section needing it. Such an arrangement will be satisfactory if the neighboring library service is conveniently located for the citizens in question and is of a quality the library feels is up to its own standards. Payment can be made in money or, if the local library can conveniently supply needs of the neighboring library, in service.

A branch library is probably the first suggestion made to the board by the community, and probably the board's own first thought. But unless the library's resources are quite ample, or a good-sized budget can be obtained for the books and staff of the new branch, a branch should be considered only as a last resort. Setting up a branch by dividing the existing book collection and the existing staff's time creates two services whose sum is weaker than the original service. In neither can a reader find the resources of materials and staff that were provided before. A branch creates new types of expenses, in addition to the cost of providing or renting space. Delivery service—involving packing, shipping, and keeping of records—is necessary. Books and requests must go back and forth; so must supplies and equipment, statistics, and memoranda. If the branch has a collection permanently located there, it will need a catalog; if the collection is on a rotating basis, records of what is sent will have to be maintained.

A bookmobile is less of a problem than a branch because it provides its own transportation. Its collection, too, should be separate and in addition to, not completely borrowed from, the main collection. A bookmobile should have a driver who can double as circulation assistant, since the bookmobile librarian should be free to give assistance to readers in selecting books and not be absorbed in circulation details. The driver is usually required to have a special driver's license and should be someone who can keep the vehicle serviced and make minor repairs. A bookmobile has the advantage of mobility. It can give service in several sections of a new area or assist in serving a second, outlying district. Locations that prove unsuccessful can easily be changed. If conditions alter, so can the bookmobile's stops.

For these reasons, the average small library in need of a second outlet may find the bookmobile rather than the branch its best solution.

Furniture

Librarians are usually more adept at selecting books than in buying furniture and equipment. In the latter as well as in the former field, however, part of the librarian's responsibility is to know what is available and what the standards are for selection.

The librarian who is fortunate enough to be able to purchase new furniture, either for a new building or for a refurbished old one, sometimes takes the line of least resistance by ordering everything from a trusted dealer's catalog. He could certainly do worse, since some libraries are completely furnished by semi-skilled local labor or by an official institution such as a prison workshop. But careful furniture selection distinguishes those items that must be built according to strict library specifications from those that can safely be selected from a wide variety of suppliers.

In considering furniture, the librarian will look for the sturdy, durable, and functional but need not settle for the unimaginative or institutional. Library supply houses of today have developed attractive lines of furniture that are a far cry from the massive and forbidding pieces of a generation or two ago. Tables and chairs need not be manufactured specifically for library use, so long as they are strong, light, and functional. Some libraries, especially small ones, use only round tables of an informal type. More often, some oblong tables suitable for study are provided, along with more informal furniture in a browsing area. Small tables, seating four or six, are often better than longer ones, as they are more easily fitted into new space arrangements and are generally preferred by readers.

Some items of furniture must be carefully made and should be purchased from a library supplier, not built locally or at a special price by a correctional institution. Among these are catalogs, shelving, and loan desks. Catalog trays must move in and out with ease, and cards must fit precisely. Shelving should be adjustable, to accommodate books of various sizes. A carefully planned loan desk is perhaps the most important piece of furniture in the library. It must suit the circulation system and whatever other work of a clerical nature done at the desk. Like the catalog, it usually contains drawers that must move easily and card trays that must be exactly the right size. If possible, the desk should be built to fit the library's own needs and specifications by an expert; if a custom-built desk is out of the question, a wisely chosen assembly from available units is the next choice.

The library's other desks need not always be "library" furniture. The highly desirable, second public service desk, at which reference and reader guidance are given, can come from a business supply house, a school supplier, or a library furniture dealer. Work space for the library's nonprofessional functions, such as mending, may be most effectively provided by built-in, shelf-type work stations along a wall. For a staff member whose work includes some typing but also much other desk work, an ordinary desk may be preferable to a special typewriter desk, which must be adjusted whenever the typewriter is needed. The typewriter can be available nearby on a wheeled typewriter stand or on a desk extension set at right angles to the desk itself.

Furniture and shelving should be appropriate to the library's general appearance and functions. Library objectives will determine what is needed, and the age and nature of the building must be taken into account. If a new building is contemplated, new furniture will naturally be selected with the new plans in mind.

Equipment and Supplies

Previous chapters have stressed the importance of staff time in the total library picture, and the need to reduce time spent on routine jobs by work simplification and the use of appropriate laborsaving equipment. As in so many other decisions, the librarian must choose a middle road in selecting or rejecting the available machines and gadgets. Some such devices, while obviously economical for a larger operation, must be scrutinized with care for the smaller library. The cost of the equipment itself, plus servicing costs, must be weighed against actual time saved; in many situations, this scrutiny will result in a reluctant admission that a particular gadget, however fascinating, makes no contribution to library efficiency.

Judicious selection of equipment requires a knowledge of what exists, an imaginative but realistic approach to its possible use, and some means of comparative evaluation of devices on the market. To learn what exists, the librarian can turn to several sources. These include:

Exhibits at American Library Association and state library association conferences. Here the librarian can actually see what is available and how it works. The sophisticated librarian will beware of being oversold by persuasive salesmen

"Goods and Gadgets" section of the *ALA Bulletin*

"Products and Equipment" section of the *Library Journal*

"Buying Guide" issue of the *Library Journal* (published annually in April)

Visits to other libraries and shoptalk with other librarians

Office-management periodicals, which frequently list supplies and equipment adaptable to library use

Requests can then be made of suppliers for catalogs of materials and equipment that look useful.

As an aid to comparative evaluation of alternatives offered, the work of the American Library Association's Library Technology Project is of great value. The Project's findings about library supplies and equipment appear in its own publications, in articles in professional journals, and in the Project's regular column in the *ALA Bulletin*. Project tests cover a wide range, from adhesives to microfilm reading machines. In addition to tests of existing products, the Project studies library needs not adequately met and supports new research to produce satisfactory materials and methods. The librarian, aware of such work in progress, will be wise to await the outcome before making a decision.

Business operations of many kinds use routines similar to those of a library. The alert librarian keeps his eyes open when he visits his bank or waits for his plane at the airport, to note how operations are managed, how work stations are set up, and how the convenience and flow of customers are provided for. Expensive study and research have gone into these arrangements, and occasionally a valuable suggestion for the library can be obtained from them.

Basic equipment for the small library will include such items as typewriters (with adequate provision for the typing of cards), shelving, bookends, charging device, and book trucks. Many small libraries need an adding machine, a microfilm reader, a drive-up book return, and a visible file for entering periodical holdings or searching reserves. Libraries with access to films will want a projector (portable) and a screen; those with recordings will want to consider a portable record player as well as earphones for the use of listeners in the library. Special shelving or tub-type recordings containers should also be considered.[1]

Coin-operated equipment sometimes can make a welcome contribution to public service at little or no cost to the library, including such items as copying machines, dispensers for pencils and pads, and public typewriters. If the library's public makes sufficient use of such dispensers and services, the owners will install, inspect, and service them and collect the money at regular intervals.

Card sorters, mending supplies, shellac, adhesive stickers, and the like are standard supply items for all libraries. In addition to the normal printed supplies necessary for circulation, overdues, reserves, and orders, the library may want to consider a supply of postcards to be sent to readers known to be interested in a subject, in order to inform them of a new book in their field. Pamphlet boxes may be needed. The small library should consider the use of rubber stamps in a number of ways besides the obvious ones of dating and identification. Considerable typing and writing by hand can be saved by a relatively inexpensive stamp. On the other hand, a stamp is uneconomical when the purchase of printed or mimeographed forms is justified by frequency of use.

For the preparation of displays ready-made letters are available; these letters may likewise be used for directional signs and section labels in the library. Standard display equipment also includes such items as a T-square, felt pens of different colors, and quick-drying paint. For inside-the-library displays, small metal book troughs or larger freestanding ones are often useful.

The items mentioned above are only a few of the most obvious needs. New supplies and methods are constantly appearing, and the librarian will want to keep in close touch with current progress and new products. If his thinking is truly service-centered and his approach to library service concentrated on improvement and development, he will recognize the contribution of modern technology toward his goals. Such a librarian, seeking and finding ways of releasing precious staff

---

[1] See Mary D. Pearson, *Recordings in the Public Library* (Chicago: A.L.A., 1963), p.44–53.

time from routines, will have no difficulty in employing the time saved in making the library a dynamic force, a delight, and a source of pride in his community.

Bibliography

American Library Association. Committee on Library Architecture and Building Planning. *Buildings for Small Public Libraries, Remodeled and Adapted, Including New Designs for Branches.* Chicago: A.L.A., 1950. 39p.

Boaz, Martha, ed. *A Living Library: Planning Public Library Buildings for Cities of 100,000 or Less; Papers Presented at an Institute on Public Library Architecture Sponsored by the School of Library Science, University of Southern California, April 25-26, 1957.* Los Angeles: Univ. of Southern California Pr., 1957. 84p.

California. State Library. "What To Do Until the Architect Comes: Planning Public Library Buildings (Proceedings of 5th Annual Institute-Workshop)," *News Notes of California Libraries,* 52: 475–632 (July, 1957).

"Commodity, Firmness and Delight: The Library Architect," *Wilson Library Bulletin,* 36:148–51 (October, 1961).

Doms, Keith. "Public Library Buildings," in Roberta Bowler, ed., *Local Public Library Administration,* p.278–312. Chicago: International City Managers' Assn., 1964.

"Effect of a New Building on Library Use," *News Notes of California Libraries,* 51:492–95 (October, 1956).

Galvin, Hoyt R. *The Small Public Library Building.* ("Public Library Manuals," no.10) Paris: UNESCO, 1959. 133p.

Goldhor, Herbert, and Sahm, Lawrence A. *The Renovation of a Medium-sized Library Building.* ("Occasional Papers," no.63) Urbana: Univ. of Illinois Graduate School of Library Science, 1961. 9p.

Messman, Howard A. *Building Materials in Library Construction.* ("Occasional Papers," no.67) Urbana: Univ. of Illinois Graduate School of Library Science, 1963. 23p.

Schunk, Russell J. *Pointers for Public Library Building Planners.* Chicago: A.L.A., 1945. 67p.

Wheeler, Joseph L. *The Effective Location of Public Library Buildings.* ("Occasional Papers," no.52) Urbana: Univ. of Illinois Graduate School of Library Science, 1958. 50p.

——— *The Small Library Building.* (Small Libraries Project Pamphlet, no.13) Chicago: A.L.A., 1963. 36p.

INDEX